武汉实验外国语学校ABCDE五步课堂教学模式丛书

丛书主编　李　茵　丛书副主编　王永汉

武汉实验外国语学校科研课题“新课程背景下初中学段高效课堂研究”

（项目编号：20084053328）

荣获武汉市科技进步三等奖

本书探究的"ABCDE五步教学模式"是该课题主要创新点之一

ABCDE五步课堂教学模式及多种教学法运用之探究

本册主编　徐　涛　蔡文静

本册副主编　李　雯　徐　佳　张家庆　梁　静

本册编者　蔡文静　陈　娅　戴文曦　董颜华
樊　娲　冯文力　何　盼　雷　佼
李　欢　李思思　李　雯　梁　静
卢　隽　彭　华　任瑶瑶　孙宇敏
向　阳　向　丹　徐　佳　徐　涛
夏涓涓　许妍琼　余　静　张冬倩
张家庆　张金霞

WUHAN UNIVERSITY PRESS

武汉大学出版社

武汉市科学技术成果《新课程背景下初中高效课堂研究》
成果登记号：wk201105003课题组成员名单

主持人：李　茵
总课题组负责人：李　茵　　王永汉
总课题组组织与联络人：余清香
总课题组代表成员：

李　茵	王永汉	余清香	徐　涛	张　玲	何幼明	周　成	李焕兰
郭　华	胡春洪	黄　莉	蒋玉涵	夏慧聪	黄　涛	殷国俊	

五个子课题研究组成员：

1、课堂教学目标的拟定及达成研究
组长：殷国俊
组员：

李　茵	余清香	胡春洪	廖艳梅	李　欢	赵　军	胡惜梅	周　翔
李思思	雷　佼	刘　青	舒荣桂	宋晓红	尹清华	黄　涛	代　欢
王　阁	王　军（历史）		张绍敏	傅　彦	陶　俊	熊采芹	

2、课堂学习方式倡导的研究
组长：张　玲
外语学科小组长：夏涓涓
组员：

袁三红	蔡文静	闵　芳	李　理	徐　菲	许妍琼	梁　静	陈海燕
李红霞	陈　娅	张冬倩	罗　娟	彭　华	钱晶晶	张家庆	雷晶艳
向　阳	向　丹	冯文力	闵　芳	徐　英	彭　华	程　颜	

3、高效课堂教师角色研究

组长：喻四明

组员：

王永汉　李焕兰　郭　华　陈　慧　夏慧聪　方晓晨　黄　莉　程　婷
杨　健　袁响雷　蔡　园　戴文曦　何　盼　王　帅　于　淼　王　倩
李　雯　柳　林　周　成　贵　杨　卢　隽　陈　力　何幼明　周　波
舒矾萍

4、高效课堂生成资源把握研究

组长:郑伟平

组员:

汪正林　张　莹　王　琛　周　丹　吴静焰　高俊文　刘有明　任瑶瑶
彭　云　李多佳　刘　燕　徐　丹　吴玉林　张金霞　潘之瑶　刘奇志

5、高效课堂教学的基本模式研究

组长:金　钊

组员：

徐　涛　陈　梅　陈颖婕　董颜华　颜　琼　周秋龄　杨　蕾　代林波
左　斌　黄　果　孙宇敏　樊　娲　周　娉　陈　明　余　静　甘　泉
王　洁　王　军(物理)　余　帆

序

如果说，一所一流的大学关注学术研究、创造精神，那么，一所一流的中学应该关注什么？

或许，98 年前的教育家蔡元培先生签署的第一部《中学校令》就能给我们以启迪：“中学以完足普通教育、造成健全国民为宗旨。”看似普通的一句话，其中却蕴含着这样的真知灼见：教育的落脚点，最后，必须落脚在学生的能力素养及健康成长上。（“完足普通教育”、“健全国民”本身就包含有个体学习能力素养、终身学习意识等多种涵义。）这与1996年国际 21 世纪教育委员会向联合国教科文组织提交的报告《教育——财富蕴藏其中》中所包含的最核心的观点“教育要使学习者学会掌握‘学习的四大支柱’”（“学会认知”、“学会做事”、“学会共同生活”和“学会生存”）有内在的关联。也与当下盛行的 PISA（Programme for International Student Assessment，国际学生评估项目，它是经济合作与发展组织的成员共同开发的项目，其目的是测试十五岁学生是否掌握了参与未来知识社会所必需的基础知识和基本技能，从而建立一套学生评价方面的教育指标）所要求的三大基本方面——阅读能力、数学能力、科学能力，以及其他诸如学习态度、学生如何管理他们的学习等方面的要求，有异曲同工之妙。他们的共同点都在于：教育的核心在于“育人”、“立人”，她必须关注“人”的能力的增强、素质的提升、道德的健全等。

如此说来，在教育的价值取向多元化的今天，一些成年人难逃教育的浮躁和功利化，重温蔡先生的这句话，对于今天的我们而言，是否会有更多的意味？

对于一所好的学校而言，除了应有较好的物质条件，但更重要的是，应该具有自己的博大胸襟和精神气质。

需要说明的是，这种精神气质和博大胸襟突出表现为：培养走向未来、具有国际视野的人才和有责任感、敢于担当的人，其教育的视野要涵盖现实，更要超越现实。关切的目光绝非只停留在作为“表层”的分数及当下，更要穿越前者，抵达“深层”的价值取向、文化积淀和更为纵深、辽阔的未来！而最能折射这种气质及视野的，我以为，体现在这所学校的方方面面，包括教学安排、课堂氛围、师生关系、社团活动、社会实践、校园环境、学校管理模式、作业布置方式及特色等。其中，学校校本课程的设置及落实，也是众多校园文化、气质承载及体现方式之一。

校本课程的设置与否，也是判断一所学校是否真的将学生的成长放在首位的参考条件之一。丰富多彩的校本课程，植根于对“新课程标准”理念的真切理解，更植根于学生群体的个体差异性和强烈求知欲的现实语境，植根于当下乃至未来的知识社会对学生能力的长远要求，更植根于学生个体终身学习的需要。它直观地展现出一所学校的精神气质和文化内涵！

作为一所具有基础性、实验性和开放性的现代化学校，我校已在多年的摸索和发展中，培养出众多活跃在外交、文化及社会各个领域的优秀人才，并逐渐形成自己特有的校园文化：“一个载体”——以外语教学为载体，“三个特色”——外语特色、开放特色、素质教育特色，五个“学生培养目标内涵”——自主精神、公民意识、科学态度、人文情怀、领袖气质。正是在这样的校园文化的指引下，武汉实验外国语学校形成了“重视学生个性发展，一切为了孩子，为了孩子的一切”的办学特色，在社会上享有较高的声誉。

作为我校特色学科的外语，自然是走在校本课程的最前列。本套“武汉实验外国语学校外语校本课程”丛书，共分为四类课程：一是阅读类，二是听力类，三是社团活动类，四是教学研讨类。

具体来说，阅读类课程选择的是我校在长期外语教学实践中，已经证实为“经典”的阅读文本，与教材呼应，同时又适度提高，是我们武汉实外学生必须要读的好读物；听力类课程是作为“武汉实外初中听力等级教程”的一部分，其中的内容既包括英语歌曲、英文演讲，也包括精彩英语对话等，内容生动，时代性突出，也贴近学生们的心灵及生活；社团活动类课程主要展现了我校的社团活动及 duty show（作者注：“值日报告比赛”——一种在课前 5 分钟，由单人或多人以小组方式展示的包含有表演、电影配音、专题探研诸如“好莱坞电影中的美国生活方式”等成果的教学活动）的精华，学生们的开阔视野和风采都让教师们感受到他们这代人的希望和茁壮成长，其中“活动现场”、“学生感悟”、“教师点评”的栏目文字能最大限度再现活动的魅力，并带给人思考的愉悦；最后一类是“教学研讨”类课程，它是我校外语教师一直坚持进行的“共同成长”教研活动过程及成果的展现，我校所有外语教师都积极参与其中，并以包括听力课、口语课、概念课、活动课等在内的多种课型，展现出了她们不同风格但却同样精彩的教学活动。

综上所述，这套校本课程是武汉实验外国语师生们精神面貌的生动再现与历史的见证。她记录并见证了一位位外语教师的辛勤善思，记录并见证一个个实外学生的可喜成长，也记录和见证了一个个外语课堂的诗意瞬间，同时，她更体现出这所学校所蕴藏的一种精神气质，一种奔跑的姿态，预示着学校更美好的发展前景。

希望这套“武汉实验外国语学校校本课程”丛书，能给予每一位读者一些触动和思考，也祝福武汉实验外国语学校的发展前景更加辉煌灿烂！

是为序。

全国人大代表
武汉市政府参事
武汉实验外国语学校校长　李茵

2011-1-17

前　言

21 世纪是一个不同国家和民族相互依赖的世界，英语已成为国际性语言，是世界科技进步、国际经济发展与文化交流的必备工具。学好一门外语，特别是英语，是知识创新和技术创新的基础，是时代和社会对于高素质人才的基本要求。

外国语学校是具有专业性教育特色的学校，它以外语教学为主要特色，同时全面发展其他学科。据权威机构评价，“外国语学校的英语教学理念新颖、内容宽厚、手段创新，是中学英语教学的最高层次，是我国英语教学的领头羊，发挥了示范性、辐射性作用”。社会上广泛使用的《看、听、学》(3L 系列教材)、《新概念英语》、《展望未来英语教程》等教材都是首先在外国语学校试用而逐步向社会推广的。

长期以来，作为全国首批七所外国语学校之一的武汉外国语学校(武汉实验外国语学校)，十分重视并高效有序地展开课程改革实验和教学方法探索工作。学校按照《国家基础教育课程改革指导纲要》的精神，从调查研究入手，贯彻“先立后破，先实验后推广”的工作方针，建立课程改革支持系统，加强对教师的培训和指导，倡导教师结合自己的教学实际进行调整和创新，鼓励学生积极探索和思考，形成了一大批教学成果。

伴随着国内中学英语教学水平的普遍提高和社会对语言学习诉求的不断增长，学校坚持引进先进教材、全英语授课、小班教学、策划开展形式多样的英语学科活动(如两年一届的外语文化节、英语剧社、原版电影配音社、外语广播台、阳光外语活动、外语角、英文卡拉 OK 比赛、英语能力竞赛、海外实践行等)，使学生在实践中拓展语言运用能力。

“ABCDE 英语高效教学模式”(以下简称“五步教学法”)以素质教育观念和教育部最新颁布的中学《英语课程标准》为依据，参照全国外国语学校 2000 年通过的《英语教学大纲》，突出“以学生为本”、“以能力为主”的理念，吸收了听说法、情景法、交际法、视听法、结构功能法、主题教学法等多种教学法的优点，根据初中学生的生理特点和本校的教学实际总结概括而成。

“五步教学法”分为“激活(Activate)、构建(Build)、养成(Cultivate)、发展(Develop)和评价(Evaluate)”五大教学步骤。其中，激活环节要求教师在课堂教学开始前的较短时间内灵活安排新颖的导入活动，促使全班学生集中注意力，迅速进入学习状态。“构建”是课堂新知识输入、新能力培养的重点环节，教师需要遵循《教学大纲》的原则和

“任务型英语教学途径”的要求，综合运用教学方法指导教学设计，营造良好的学习氛围，使学生快乐、自然、轻松、有效地学习语言。“养成”是对“构建”环节的强化，需要教师按照启发式教学原则，设计饶有趣味的训练来充分调动学生学习的主动性，实现教师主导作用和学生主体作用的结合、系统知识学习与智力充分发展的结合、书本知识和直接经验的结合，帮助学生加强对新知识、新能力的掌握。“发展”环节要求教师科学地安排课堂时间，创新设计真实语言环境来综合概括“构建”及“养成”所传达的语言信息，巩固课堂教学、衔接新旧知识、贯通前后内容，帮助学生学习训练，复习巩固。“评价”环节包括获取与处理学生对每节课知识的了解程度和对语言技能掌握程度的反馈、教师教育方法和教育技巧等信息，检测评估教学活动的实际效果，帮助教师及时总结经验，调控教学活动，指导学生分析学习成效，调整学习策略，排除学习障碍。

“五步教学法”教学模式具有如下特点。

(1)指导性：该教学法对于教师组织教学提出了四方面的具体要求，即语言教学应与文化背景、国情知识介绍相结合；充分调动学生的学习主动性和积极性；利用多媒体等现代教学手段提高语言教学质量；注重把握特点、确定重点，多方综合、相互促进，相对集中、注意适度，突出主体、培养能力。

(2)综合性：“五步教学法”教学模式体现了启发式的教学思想，融合了多种教学法的优点，符合武汉实际，具有外校特色。教师可以根据教材、学生、时间、教学环境和教学目标的不同综合灵活使用，以达到教学效果的最优化。

(3)服务性：“五步教学法”是以学生为主体设计的教学模式，目的是为了给学生创设生动丰富的语言学习环境，在课堂教学中充分尊重、维持和培养不同学生的学习策略，激发他们内在的学习动机，指导、帮助他们圆满完成学习任务。

(4)实用性：“五步教学法”理念新颖，内容详尽，体系完整，实用性强，不仅对于外国语学校教师的专业成长具有指导性，对于普通中学的英语教师也具有参考作用。

本书具体介绍武汉外国语学校(武汉实验外国语学校)的“ABCDE 英语高效教学模式”英语课实例，从课堂教学的实际过程来分析“ABCDE 五步法”教学模式的高效性。

我们深深感到，对于中学英语教学模式和方法的探索永无止境。由于我们学识浅薄，加之时间仓促，本书难免存在不少问题，恳请同行专家赐教指正。

本书特邀请到武汉大学外国语言文学学院靳奇老师担任主审。在本书的编写过程中，靳奇老师百忙中全程参与审订工作并提出了很多宝贵的审订意见及建议，在此表示衷心感谢。

附注：“五步教学法”每个步骤的名称在本书中将简化，例如将“激活(Activate)环节”简称为“(A)环节”。

课　例

课例 1：《展望未来》第一册第一单元 International English

授课教师：徐　涛　武汉实验外国语学校外事办公室主任、英语教师，中央电视台“希望之星”英语大赛湖北赛区评委会主席，武汉市优秀青年教师，学校英语学科带头人，曾多次参与武汉市中考英语试卷命题，曾荣获武汉市优质课大赛一等奖并多次荣获全国和省市其他奖励。

【课例 1】　把教学材料和学生实际情况做了一番有机整合，在(A)环节中省略一般的话题热身，而是直接播放一段关于机场的教学视频，视频结束后让学生回忆他们看到的事物并把相关词汇归类。课堂设计既有趣味性，又有综合性，很适合学生的学习程度和特点。接着，教师把(B)、(C)两个环节相结合，通过听、说来熟悉课文，对话提问进而强化与国籍、国家、首都相关的词汇和句型，巩固所学知识。(D)环节的设计上，教师充分利用教材提供的含有信息差的资料，组织学生进行小组活动，语境真实可信，根据学生个体实际分别提出要求，练习到位又能启发每一个学生。(E)环节贯穿于活动的方方面面，最终学生能展示出流利的语言和包容合作的精神。

课例 2：《综合英语》第四册第八单元 Street Accident

授课教师：卢　隽　武汉实验外国语学校英语教师，武汉市优秀青年教师，曾荣获全国英语优质课一等奖和湖北省武汉市英语优质课一等奖等多项荣誉。

【课例 2】　利用本节课适逢圣诞前夕这个现实条件，用圣诞老人的交通工具这个话题激活课堂，既自然又高效，符合(A)环节简短、灵活、新颖的要求。在理解篇章的过程中，分层次，抓结构，突破难句。对于充斥很多生词的文章，不奢求面面俱到，而是把握整体结构，着眼关键句中的关键词汇及用法，通过设置紧凑且层次分明的任务达到让学生从理解重难点词句到试着运用它们的目的，(B)环节非常扎实。紧接着，课堂提供了外媒语料，原汁原味，学生实际运用和体验了在前一个环节中学到的点读和扫读技巧。这个(C)环节不但做到了知识和技能的强化，又开拓了学生的视野，把语言回归现实。最后的(D)环节让学生回归当下，让学生以小组为单位，合作讨论并完成由读向写的过渡——“如何避免交通事故”。

在课堂教学进行的过程中，贯穿(E)环节，及时给予学生简洁而直接的评价，教师对于学生的各种看法和观点应该采取包容的态度，但同时要明确地表明自己的观点，以此营造交流的氛围。不敷衍、不曲解、不抹杀与己相悖的想法，使学生自然地将表达的重点从语言结构上转移到语言内容上。

这节和写作紧密连接的阅读课，构思巧妙，安排得当，学生接受度高，激活和发展环节当属亮点，把一节普通的英语课紧密地和生活联系在一起，学生不但能掌握英语知识，学会阅读和写作技巧，同时也开始思考关怀生命的问题。

课例3：《新目标》八年级上册第八单元 Section A How Was Your School Trip

授课教师：张家庆 武汉实验外国语学校英语教师，学校英语备课组长，曾荣获湖北省英语优质课说课一等奖和武汉市英语优质课一等奖等多项荣誉。

【课例3】 本次课的教学对象是来自武汉市武昌某中学初二年级的学生。根据这节课的目标、性质和教学对象等的特点，在(A)环节中，教师通过一组近期在英国游学的照片吸引学生的注意力，并简单介绍了自己，拉近了与陌生教学对象的距离，为授课奠定了良好的互动基础。

这节课的(B)环节要围绕摸清学生的基础，让学生适应新老师，以传授新知识和为下一个环节做铺垫等目的进行，设计的可伸缩性比较强。教师通过细化英国游学的具体活动和观看外教示范视频两个环节来逐步加深知识构建的范围及程度，从鼓励学生简单地说“是与否”积极回应过渡到整句模仿，直至独立回答，过渡自然，练习到位。本课的(C)环节使用启发的方式让学生体会和模仿，教师将阅读资料改编为一段对话，并将外教的表演录制成视频，通过让学生观看这段视频完成判断正误和排序两个英语活动，请学生结合课本文章和图片进行复述。由于生词和词组也在构建环节得以学习，所以大部分学生在本环节能够比较顺利地将所学课文复述出来，促进学生建立学习英语的信心和兴趣。在(D)环节中，教师设计小组活动时用问答形式来解决一个悬疑问题，有趣又有效。最后，教师组织学生进行英语活动，纠正了学生在语言练习中容易犯的错误，复习了本节课的学习内容，布置了课后作业(E)。

整节课以活动贯穿始终，学生在参与英语活动中不知不觉地学习并掌握了新知识。活动设计由简到繁，环环相扣，既不重复，也不简单枯燥，学生获得了完成任务后的兴奋感和成就感。

课例4：《新目标》七年级上册第五单元3a-4 Section A

授课教师：李　欢　武汉实验外国语学校英语教师，曾荣获湖北省英语优质课说课一等奖等多项荣誉。

【课例4】　是一节听说课。在(A)环节中，教师设计的“猜猜看”游戏，既复习了句型，又导入到新的话题“球类运动”中去。

(B)和(C)环节是这节课的亮点。教师按照听、说、读、写的认知规律和难度设计了由浅入深的不同任务。首先，学生带着问题听小对话，进而边听边填写空缺单词。接着，学生通过目标语言的输入和新学单词的使用来进一步感知语言；通过完成不同难易层次的任务构建对目标语言的理解，练习要求掌握的单词和了解目标语言的文化背景及内涵。然后，要求学生大声朗读文本材料，并以朗读材料为基本框架，根据图片自己组织对话。这是一个使用语言的过程，也是对学习内容进一步强化的过程。

这节课中，不同层次的学生在整堂课中都能够得到训练。学生在获取知识的过程中充分培养了团体合作的精神，并建立了自信。教师能够通过课堂教学和课后作业完成对学生语言技能、情感态度和学习策略的引导(E)。

课例5：《展望未来》第二册第八单元 Is It Wrong to Eat Meat?

授课教师：徐　佳　武汉实验外国语学校英语教师，曾荣获全国“创新教育与实验”课题研究成果一等奖和厦门市第三届中学课堂教学改革创新大赛一等奖等多项荣誉。

【课例5】　是一节以阅读为基础训练学生思辨能力的综合课，单元话题是饮食，目标阅读文章是素食主义。针对有一定自学能力的初三学生，教师在(A)环节中不平铺直叙，而是直接切入素食主义这个重点话题，在复习句型热身的基础上，自然地介绍了重点生词的意思和用法(B)。在你来我往的问答过程中，培养学生逐渐养成思考和表达的习惯和能力(C)，为最后的辩论活动做铺垫。辩论活动中学生巩固了前面环节所学到形容词，又加入了自己的独立想法，任何表达都得到聆听，语言使用上的不规范也能得到修正(E)。最后，教师通过增加的阅读材料把课堂话题提升到健康饮食的角度，既正视人们不同的饮食选择，又倡导科学的生活方式(D)。

“ABCDE 五步教学法”具有很强的指导性，也有灵活修改的空间。不一定每节课都要完整体现 ABCDE 每一个步骤，这也不是“五步教学法”所要求的。在实际的教学过程中，英语教师面对自己特定的教学对象和教学材料，可以灵活运用不同的教学理论和教学方式，以达到最佳的教学效果。

目录
Contents

五步课堂教学模式

UNIT 1

International English

BY 徐涛
2011/03/06

Ⅰ Teaching Objectives:

1. Students are required to master the following words and useful expressions

piano (n); video cassette (n); disco (n); toilet (n); restaurant (n); hamburger (n); violin (n); hotel (n); reception (n); saxophone (n); cassette (n); camera (n); arrivals (n pl); bus stop (n); camera (n); capital (n); departure (n pl); diary (ies) (n); dollar (n); double (adj); facility (ies) (n); guidebook (n); information (n); international (adj); jazz (n); map (n); meal (n); minute (n); nationality (ies) (n); nightclub (n); passport (n); postcard (n); poster (n); pound (n); private (adj); single (adj); souvenir (n); tourist office (n).

2. Focus

Countries, nationalities and capital cities; Asking meaning; Facilities; Money (British and American); Buying things.

3. Functional language

Talking about names, countries and nationalities; Talking about places; Talking about objects; Greeting; Asking about meaning; Buying things.

Ⅱ Teaching Aids:

Tape recorder; Slide show; Picture show.

Ⅲ Key Points:

1. Dialogue presentation
2. Vocabulary and grammar usage in real-situation dialogues
3. Free dialogue making
4. Learn the expressions used at the airport

CONTENTS

Ⅳ Teaching Procedures:

STEP I ACTIVATE

1. Greeting and duty report
2. Guessing game:
   a) Ask the students to remember the items after watching the video;
   b) Ask the students to classify the words in the part "Welcome to English".

STEP 2 BUILD

1. Presentation

Tell the students that we are going to learn the dialogues of first meeting and dialogues at the airport.

2. Listening

Now listen to the dialogue and find out this information.

(1) What's the man's name?
(2) Where is he?

(1) This is the first meet of James and Marco. (T/F)
(2) Teresa knows both James and Marco. (T/F)

(1) Where does the man come from?
(2) Where is the woman from?

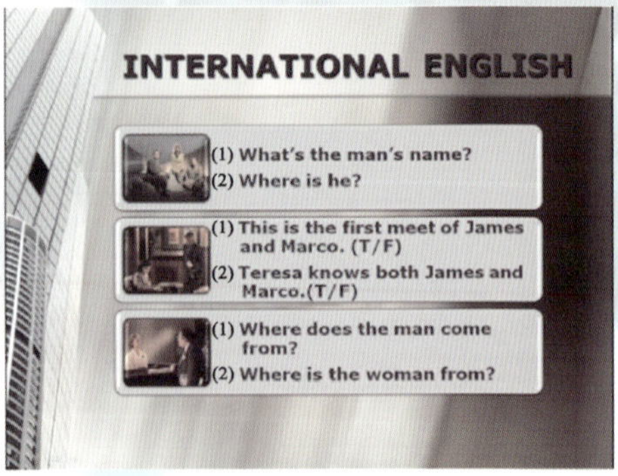

STEP 3 CULTIVATE

1. New Words

COUNTRY	NATIONALITY	CAPITAL
The United States	American	Washington D. C.
Japan	Japanese	Tokyo
Britain	British	London
France	French	Paris
Germany	German	Berlin
Greece	Greek	Athens
Ireland	Irish	Dublin
Italy	Italian	Rome
Poland	Polish	Warsaw
Portugal	Portuguese	Lisbon
Spain	Spanish	Madrid
Turkey	Turkish	Ankara
Australia	Australian	Canberra
Egypt	Egyptian	Cairo

2. Listening

(1) Passport
(2) Facilities
(3) Announcements

3. Activities

(1) Places
(2) Shop
(3) Guessing

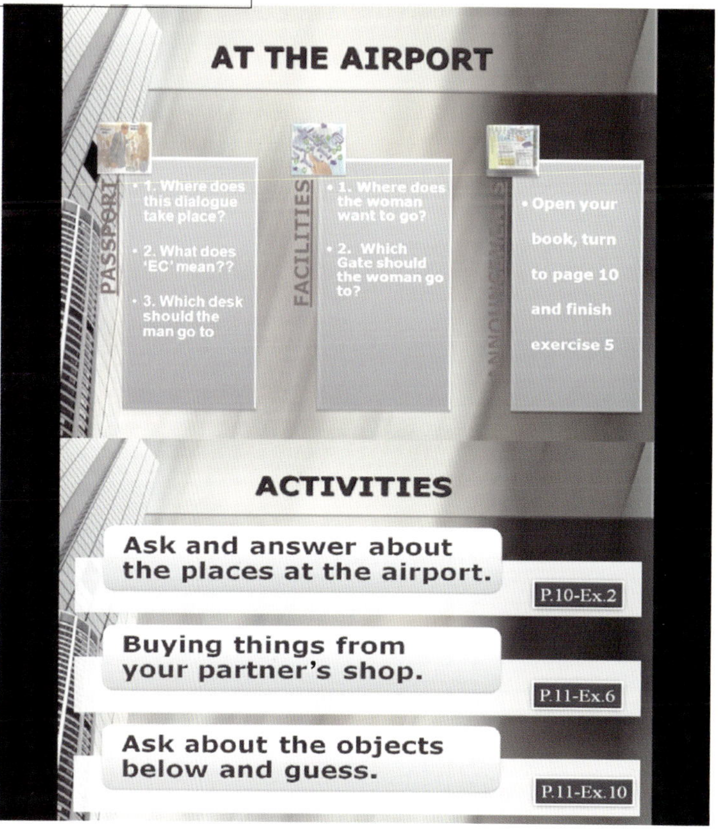

SKILLS

Listening (T.B.-p12.1)	Speaking (T.B.-p12.3)
Reading (T.L.-p8.VIII)	Writing (T.L.-p4.II-V)

Teaching Plan of Unit 8
IEC Book VI

教师：卢隽

Teaching Aims:

1. Do some reading and understand the passage.
2. Learn some useful words and expressions.
3. Encourage the students to express their ideas of the topic.

Teaching Objects:

25 students from Grade Nine.

Language Points:

1. How to describe accidents on road.
2. Find the key information from reports/news.

Teaching Aids:

A computer and a tape.

Teaching Methods:

A comprehensive teaching approach in intensive reading.

Teaching Procedures

	1. Regular greetings and warming-up activity. 2. Lead in. Listen to part of a Christmas song and answer the questions. Listen to the mini-conversations between the teacher and one of the students.

*A*ctivate

在课堂教学开始前的较短时间内灵活安排新颖的导入活动，促使全班学生集中注意力，迅速进入学习状态。

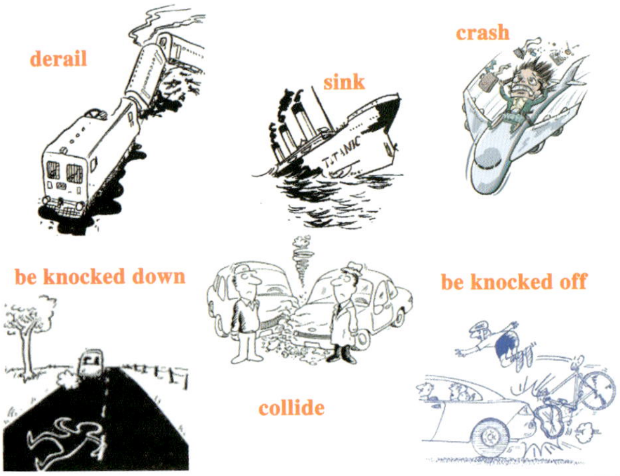

*B*uild

运用综合教学方法指导教学设计，营造良好的学习氛围，使学生快乐、自然、轻松、有效地学习语言。

3. Reading.

Read the passage and complete the tasks.

(1) Understand the new words and expressions.

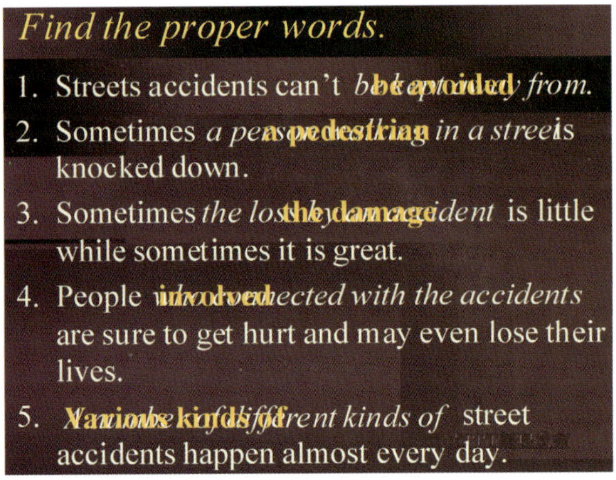

(2) Answer the questions and know how to find the proper information in the passage.

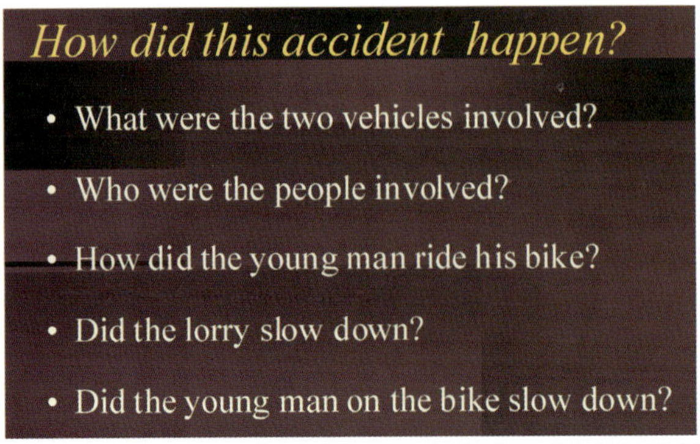

Cultivate

按照启发式教学原则，设计饶有趣味的训练来充分调动学生学习的主动性。

(3) Read the supplementary material.

Olden Times

no.203.078 THE WORLDS OLDEST NEWSPAPER - since 1879 -

Forever 15

Ryan Didone

Ryan Didone was a typical, fun-loving teenager. He liked sports, riding his dirt bike and spending time with his friends and family.

But all that changed in a matter of minutes in the fall of 2008. Ryan and four of his friends were riding in a car when the driver lost control and bumped into a tree.

The accident caused terrible injuries to all the people involved. Ryan was flown to a nearby hospital, where he died a short time later. He was 15 years old. Capt.Thomas Didone, Ryan's father, says the crash that took his son's life was a direct result of distracted driving.

It is this tragic story that made him spend many years of his life teaching teenagers and their families about safe driving.

Develop

设计真实的语言环境来综合概括构建及养成部分所传达的语言信息，巩固课堂教学、衔接新旧知识、贯通前后内容，帮助学生学习训练，复习巩固。

4. Group discussion.

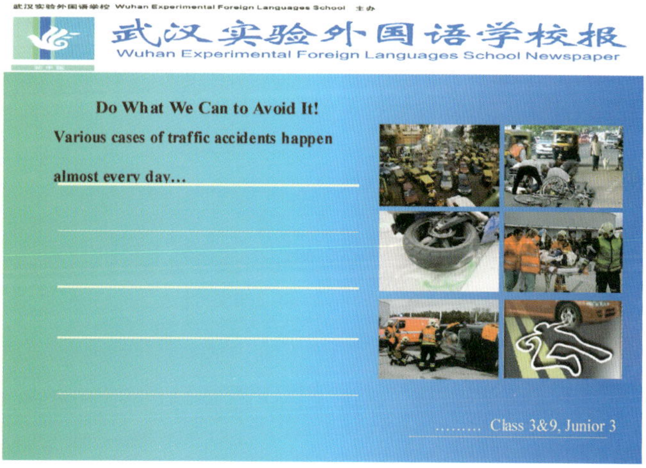

Evaluate

评估教学活动的实际效果，分析学习成效，帮助学生排除学习障碍。

5. Presentation and comments.

6. Homework setting.

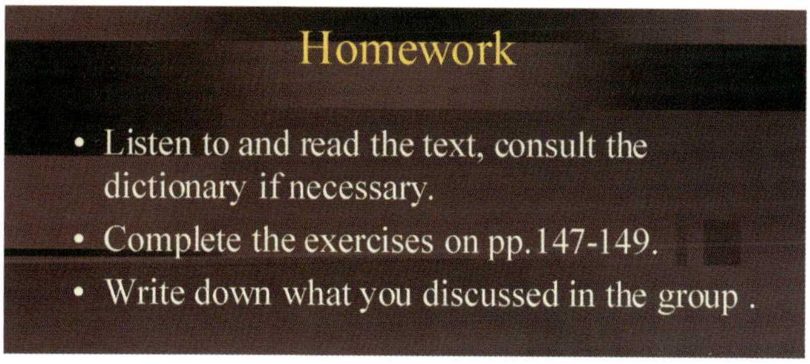

课程设计及反思

教师：卢隽

我的这节课选取了《全国外国语学校综合英语教程》第四册第八单元的阅读部分 Street Accidents 一文，是一节阅读课，目的在于帮助学生在准确理解文章的基础上，接触并感受点读和扫读的阅读技巧，并加以运用。

下面就对本节课的具体操作加以说明。

在 warming up 部分，结合授课时正处于圣诞节前夕的实际，从讨论圣诞老人的交通工具入手，将相关词语及表达呈现给学生。

在理解篇章的过程中，分层次，抓结构，突破难句。本文篇幅较长，生词及表达均占一定比重，因此在处理的过程中，不奢求面面俱到，而是把握整体结构，着眼关键句中的关键词汇及其用法。

在运用点读、扫读方法的过程中，引导和鼓励学生处理信息，化繁为简。在材料的选择上全部采用原汁原味的外媒消息，尽可能展现相关话题在实际生活中的真实面貌。

在回归话题、拓展思维过程中，围绕学生已获得的信息，以 pair work 或 team work 的活动形式，鼓励学生主动挑选应用所学知识，由读向写过渡，完成书面表达的课内任务。

☞ 课堂反思：

这节课基本实现了课前设定的目标。课堂推进迅速而流畅，从课堂内学生的反应来看，理解课文、增加词汇、围绕本话题提出自己的想法和建议这些目标均已实现。

在 Activate 阶段，学生对于书信问答引出生词的活动感到很新鲜，注意力迅速集中到了本节课的话题上。因此，好的热身活动必不可少，且值得教师花足心思。

在课程进行的过程中，贯穿 Evaluate，及时给予学生简洁直接的评价，教师对于学生的各种看法和观点应该采取包容的态度，但同时要明确地表明自己的观点，以此营造交流的氛围。不敷衍、不曲解、不抹杀与己相悖的想法，使学生自然地将表达的重点从语言结构上转移到语言内容上，最终实现语言的工具作用。

如果在时间安排上将热身部分的节奏加快，将拓展阅读部分稍做整合，这样可以使学生们在自由表达观点以及其后的书面化阶段时间更充裕。

Teaching Plan of Unit 8
Section A *Go for it!* Junior 2

教师：张家庆

Teaching Aims:

1. To get the students to know the past tense of verbs.
2. To get them to know how to use different questions to ask about the things happened in the past.

Teaching Objects:

The students from Junior 2.

Language Points:

Sentence patterns:

Did you go to...? Yes, I did. /No, I didn't. I went to ...

Were there any...? Yes, there were. /No, there weren't.

Teaching Aids:

PowerPoint slides, handouts, and notes on board.

Teaching Methods:

1. Audio-visual Method.
2. Communicative Approach.
3. Task-based Approach.

Teaching Procedures

Activate

在课堂教学开始前的较短时间内灵活安排新颖的导入活动，促使全班学生集中注意力，迅速进入学习状态。

1. Greetings.
2. Show the students some pictures about the teacher's school trip in 2009 by doing a game with photos.

Build

运用综合教学方法指导教学设计，营造良好的学习氛围，使学生快乐、自然、轻松、有效地学习语言。

Ask the students to work in pairs to practice the sentences as the examples from the videos.

*C*ultivate

按照启发式教学原则，设计饶有趣味的训练来充分调动学生学习的主动性。

1. Listen and finish the exercises.
2. Watch the video and finish the exercises.
3. Watch the video again and ask the students to try to retell the dialogue.

*D*evelop

设计真实的语言环境来综合概括构建及养成部分所传达的语言信息，巩固课堂教学、衔接新旧知识、贯通前后内容，帮助学生学习训练，复习巩固。

The teacher divides the class into 4-6 groups. Ask them to find out the person who broke the window yesterday evening by asking questions.

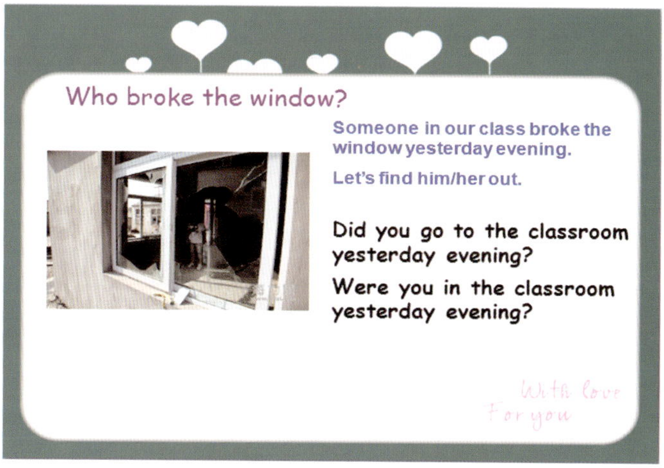

	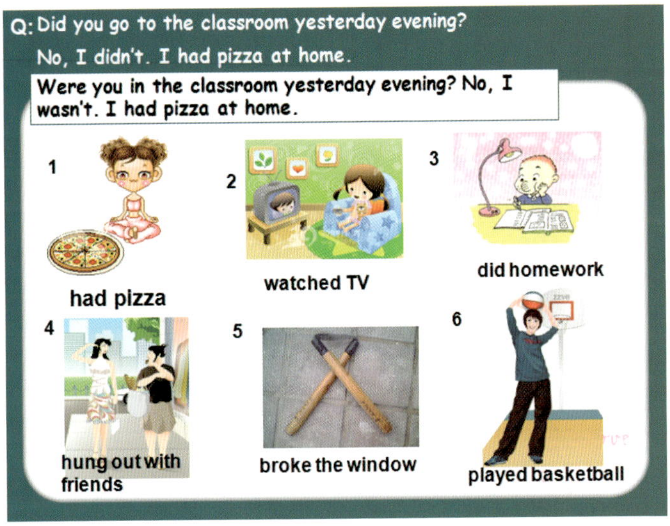
*E*valuate 评估教学活动的实际效果，分析学习成效，帮助学生排除学习障碍。	The teacher gives some good advice of the activity. And give them the homework. 

课程设计及反思

张家庆

本节课是一节武汉市教学展示课，教学对象是来自湖北省水果湖第二中学初二年级的学生。教学内容是人教版《新目标》八年级上册第八单元 Section A 部分，主要讲解的是一般过去时在英语表达中的运用，是一节任务型教学法贯穿始终的展示课。

1. 激活(Activate)　在课堂开始前的一分钟，我简单地向同学们介绍了我自己，然后通过一组我自己在英国拍的照片吸引学生的注意力，让学生们对我在 2009 年的一次游学经历产生兴趣。

2. 构建(Build)　在这一环节我遵循《教学大纲》的原则和“任务型英语教学途径”的要求，设计了一个 TRUE OR FALSE 的小游戏，让学生对我游学经历的具体活动进行判断。学生对我的亲身经历和异国文化与建筑十分感兴趣，全班学生都积极地参与进来。完成游戏之后我马上就学生在游戏环节读到的句子要求学生运用一般过去时的一般疑问句形式、否定形式和肯定形式进行练习。在练习之前我还让学生观看了一段我请英语外教做练习示范的视频，让学生从视听直观感受，在听、说、读三方面进行练习。与此同时英语外教的示范视频也能使学生产生兴趣，十分愿意按小组进行口头练习，最后学生参与度很高，十分愿意向大家展示自己的英语口语。在整个构建的过程中，我结合了本节课的生词和词组，学生在游戏和练习的过程中已经能够理解和熟练运用这些单词和词组了。

3. 养成(Cultivate)　对构建环节的强化，需要教师按照启发式教学原则，设计饶有趣味的训练来充分调动学生学习的主动性，实现教师主导作用和学生主体作用的结合、系统知识学习与智力充分发展的结合、书本知识和直接经验的结合，帮助学生加强对新知识、新能力的掌握。在这一环节我将阅读资料改编为一段对话，并将英语外教的表演录制成视频，通过让学生观看这段视频完成判断正误和排序两个英语活动。最后请学生结合课本文章和图片进行复述。由于生词和词组也在构建环节中得到学习，所以在复述环节大部分学生能够比较顺利地将所学习的课文复述出来，也能很好地建立学生学习英语的信心和兴趣。

4. 发展(Develop)　在这一环节我设计了一个英语活动，让学生通过运用一般过去时的疑问句形式找出打破窗户的人。

5. 评价(Evaluate)　在这节课的最后我评价了学生的英语活动，纠正了学生在语言练习中容易犯的错误，复习了本节课的学习内容，最后布置了课后作业。

☞ 教学反思：

任务型教学法以任务组织教学，在任务的履行过程中，以参与、体验、互动、交流、合作的学习方式，充分发挥学习者自身的认知能力，调动他们已有的目的语资源，在实践中感知、认识、应用目的语，在“干”中学，在“用”中学。通过有趣的课堂交际活动有效地激发学习者的学习动机，使他们主动参与学习。

整节课以活动贯穿始终，学生在完成一个又一个的英语活动中不知不觉地学习并掌握了这节课的新知识。活动与活动之间既不重复，也不简单枯燥，而是由简到繁，环环相扣，使学生获得完成任务后的兴奋感和成就感。

Teaching Plan of *Go for it!* 七年级 Unit 5 Section A 3a-4

教师：李欢

Teaching Aims:

1. To get the students to ask and answer questions about ownership.
2. To get the students to make suggestions.
3. To get the students to work in groups.

Teaching Objects:

Grade Seven.

Language Points:

1. Let's do…
2. I don't have…

Teaching Aids:

Tape recorder, slide show, and picture show.

Teaching Methods:

1. Communicative Approach.
2. Task-based Approach.

Teaching Procedures

Activate

在课堂教学开始前的较短时间内灵活安排新颖的导入活动，促使全班学生集中注意力，迅速进入学习状态。

Step 1 Greeting and self-introduction.
I'll tell the students my English name and Chinese name, and I will ask theirs. In this step, I'll remind them about the difference between the expressing ways of Chinese name and English name.

Step 2 Guessing game.
I'll tell the students something more about myself. I'll let the them guess which city I'm from by the given words: Hubei, hot, big. It's clear the answer is Wuhan.
We'll continue the game by giving them more words about sports, for example:

	Key Words		**Answers**
1. Hubei	Hot	Big	Wuhan
2. 2006	Germany	Beckham	Soccer
3. China	Deng Yaping	Small	Ping-pong
4. Racket	Australia	Williams	Tennis
5. Cap	Glove	Bat	Baseball
6. China	Lang Ping	Net	Volleyball
7. America	Yao Ming	NBA	Basketball

Step 3 After the students guess out the sports name, I'll put the pictures of several ball sports on the blackboard.

Step 4 In this part, I'll let the students read the new words together.
New words: soccer bat tennis racket volleyball

Build

运用综合教学方法指导教学设计，营造良好的学习氛围，使学生快乐、自然、轻松、有效地学习语言。

Step 1 After the guessing game, the students will listen to 3 dialogues about sports.

Tapescript	**Questions**
1. A: Let's play soccer.	
B: That sounds good!	What do they play?
2. A: Let's play basketball.	
B: No, I don't have a basketball.	
A: Let's play tennis.	What do they play at last?
B: That sounds good!	
3. A: Let's play tennis.	
B: I don't have a tennis racket.	
A: Let's play volleyball.	What do they play at last?
B: That sounds good!	

Step 2 Fill in the blanks.
I'll ask the students to open their books to fill in the blanks in 3a with the information they have got in the listening part in Step 1, and tell the teacher which sport is played at last.

Cultivate 按照启发式教学原则，设计饶有趣味的训练来充分调动学生学习的主动性。	Read, role-play and pair work. I'll let the students read the dialogues in 3a and 3b, then practice the dialogue in 3b with the 4 pictures in the textbook in pairs. At last, I'll check their dialogues.
Develop 设计真实的语言环境来综合概括构建及养成部分所传达的语言信息，巩固课堂教学、衔接新旧知识、贯通前后内容，帮助学生学习训练，复习巩固。	Step 1 I'll divide the students into groups. The students in each group will ask questions about the information given in the card in Ex. 4. Step 2 I'll let the students tell me how many students play each sport. I'll choose the sport which most students chose. Take BASEBALL as an example. I'll tell the students we'll have a baseball club. Step 3 I'll tell the whole class to design a poster for the baseball club and show it on the blackboard.
Evaluate 评估教学活动的实际效果，分析学习成效，帮助学生排除学习障碍。	Step 4 I'll let the group leader of each group to give a very short speech for their group according to their posters, and try to call as many students as possible to join their club. The group which gets the most club members is the winner. Homework The students are asked to ask 5 students in other groups about the card in Ex. 4, and write a survey.

Notes:

Design of the Blackboard

Unit 5 Do you have a soccer ball?

Vocabulary: Racket

Ball Games:

Ping-pong

Tennis

Soccer

Volleyball

Basketball

Baseball

Key Structures:

1. Let's play ________.
2. I don't have ________.
3. That sounds good.

The Poster of Our Sports Club

课程设计及反思

教师：李欢

我的这节课选取了 *Go for it* 七年级上第五单元的 3a-4 Section A 部分，是一节听说课。

我这节课的教学目的：一、学生通过对文本的学习了解和掌握球类运动的说法。二、学生通过课堂教学活动掌握物品所属关系的说法。在教学过程中，我主要使用了任务型教学法。

在导入部分(Warming up)，我使用了任务型教学法。教师通过自我介绍使学生更好地了解授课教师，为在之后的教学过程中师生能够良好互动奠定基础。在此过程中，教师带领学生复习 first name 及 last name 并引出 guessing game 进而使学生了解球类运动的名称。教师通过此环节充分调动学生的学习兴趣，激发学生的学习热情。(A)

在课程主体部分(Presentation)，我同样也使用了任务型教学法。在这个环节中教师按照听、说、读、写的认知规律设置了难度由浅入深的不同任务。在第一步和第二步中，学生带着问题听小对话，进而边听边填写空缺单词。学生通过目标语言的输入和新学单词的使用来进一步感知语言。学生在课堂学习的过程中通过完成不同难易层次的任务构建了对目标语言的理解，练习了要求掌握的单词和句型，了解了目标语言的文化背景及内涵(B)。在课程主体部分的第三步中，教师要求学生大声朗读文本材料，并要求学生以朗读材料为基本框架根据图片自己组织对话。这是一个使用语言的过程，也是对学习内容进一步强化的过程。(C)

完成课堂教学主体部分后，教师根据学生学习和练习的情况安排拓展部分(Development)。教师设置了符合学生兴趣爱好、能够激发学生学习热情的任务活动，帮助学生使用目标语言，并运用目标语言进行思维活动。(D)

在拓展部分的最后一个步骤中，教师要求学生通过小组活动的展示和小组间的竞争，在真实的交际中使用目标语言，教师依据活动结果对学生进行评价。在家庭作业部分，教师要求学生通过“写”的学习方式复习巩固课内所学内容。教师通过批改作业对学生的学习情况进行评价。以上两种评价方式能够使教师较为直接地了解学生对所学内容的掌握情况。(E)

在这节课中，教师使用任务型教学法完成了整体的教学任务。在教学过程中，教师按照听、说、读、写的认知规律设置了不同难度的任务，能够使学生在循序渐进的过程中完成目标语言的学习。同时，不同层次的学生在整堂课中都能够得到训练。学生在获取知识的过程中充分培养了团体合作的精神，并建立了自信。教师能够通过课堂教学和课后作业完成对学生语言技能、情感态度和学习策略的引导。

Teaching Plan of *Look Ahead* B2 Unit 8 Is It Wrong to Eat Meat?

教师：徐佳

Teaching Aims:

1. The students are able to tell different meat and other food categories.
2. The students can understand the difference between vegans and vegetarians.
3. The students can tell why some people become vegetarians and vegans.
4. The students can express their opinions about food.

Teaching Objects:

Target students are junior three students. Their English levels and skills are relatively better. They are eager to know something new and express themselves. It's better to provide them real materials rather than faked ones during study. That's why I searched through the Internet to find out true stories about animal factory farming. Considering the students are only teenagers, I omitted the bloody news and pictures. Luckily, the main text of the book is real, too.

Language Points:

Nouns: vegetarian, vegan, dairy product, peppers, lettuce
Adjectives: disgusted, sick, natural
Verbs: suffer, disgust
Phrases: in bad conditions, as well as
Structures: I think/feel... I don't think...

Teaching Aids:

All the tools needed are PPT, blackboard and chalk.

Teaching Methods:

To motivate the students to develop their reading and speaking skills, individual speaking questions, conversational questions and discussing are arranged. Activities include role play, comparison, etc.

1. Task-based Language Teaching Approach.
2. Communicative Approach.
3. Motivation Strategies(动机激发策略).
4. Vocabulary Teaching Strategies(词汇教学策略).

Teaching Procedures

Activate

在课堂教学开始前的较短时间内灵活安排新颖的导入活动，促使全班学生集中注意力，迅速进入学习状态。

1. Encourage the students to tell different kinds of meat and animals' names.

T： Every day we eat some meat. Can you tell me what kinds of meat we usually eat?

Ss： Port (pig), beef (cow), lamb (sheep), fish, etc.

T： Some people sometimes eat other animals, like...

Ss： Dogs, donkeys, rabbits and snakes.

T： Have you ever tasted dogs/rabbits?

Ss： Not very often. / Never. /Yes.

T： Do you usually eat pork/beef?

Ss： Yes.

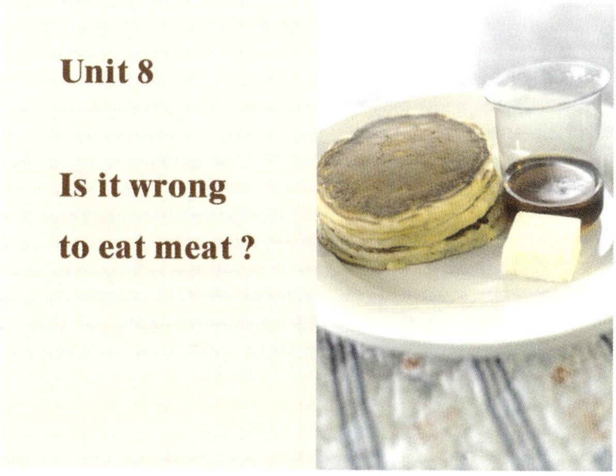

2. Talking about how animals are kept and killed. Lead out some key points.

T: Why don't many of you/ people often eat dogs/rabbits?
Have you seen how people kill it? Can you imagine? How do you feel?

Ss: Awful/ Terrible/Disgusting.

T: Do people keep and kill pigs in the same way?
(Show some pictures.)

Ss: It makes me sick. /I feel very sick.
I feel disgusted. / It's disgusting.
They are kept in bad conditions.

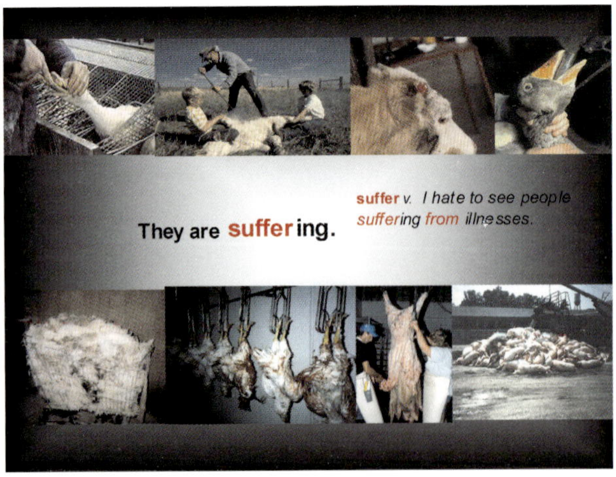

***B*uild**

运用综合教学方法指导教学设计，营造良好的学习氛围，使学生快乐、自然、轻松、有效地学习语言。

3. Turn to the text.

T: Because of this, some people don't want to eat meat any more. They become vegetarians. A few people even think they can't eat milk, cheese and eggs (dairy products) any more. Because they have something to do with the animals. We call them vegans. Danni is a vegan now. But Brian feels differently about food. How do they think?

Read the text and find out.

4. General questions.

① What's the difference between their eating habits?

② What can't a vegetarian eat? What can't a vegan eat?

5. More detailed questions. Encourage the students to retell the content.

Part 1　True or false.

① Danni is an American singer. (F)

② She doesn't eat meat and fish only. (F)

③ She stopped eating meat because it makes her feel sick. (T)

④ She gave up fish because it's bad for her voice. (T)

⑤ She got to know the facts about farm animals on TV. (F)

⑥ Becoming a vegan is good for her and the animals. (T)

Part 2　Questions about Brain.

⑦ What food does Brian like?

Meat, junk food, burger, chicken takeaways.

⑧ What food doesn't he like?

Tomatoes, crispy lettuce, green peppers, onions.

⑨ How does he feel about eating meat?

Natural.

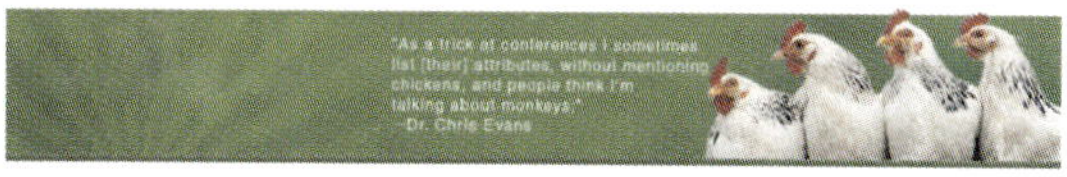

Some people can't stand this. They choose to give up eating animals. They become *vegetarians*.

Some even give up those food related to animals, like eggs and *dairy products*. They become *vegans*.

Cultivate

按照启发式教学原则，设计饶有趣味的训练来充分调动学生学习的主动性。

Will you choose to become
a vegetarian or a vegan?

Is it wrong to eat meat?

General questions.

① What is the difference between their eating habits?

② What can't a vegetarian eat?
What can't a vegan eat?

True or false.
(Correct the mistakes.)

①Danni is an American singer. *F*

②She doesn't eat meat and fish only. *F*

③She stopped eating meat because it makes her feel sick. *T*

④She gave up fish because it's bad for her voice. *F*

⑤She got to know the facts about farm animals on TV. *F*

⑥Becoming a vegan is good for her and the animals. *T*

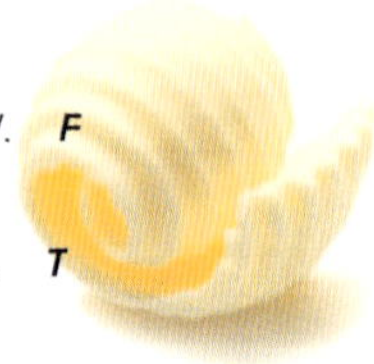

Questions about Brain:

① What food does he like?

② What food doesn't he like?

③ How does he feel about eating meat?

Natural. nature *n.*
natural *adj.*
naturally *adv.*

Develop

设计真实的语言环境来综合概括构建及养成部分所传达的语言信息，巩固课堂教学、衔接新旧知识、贯通前后内容，帮助学生学习训练，复习巩固。

6. Why does he think it's natural? Is it wrong to eat meat? Page 61 Ex. 6 Match

for	against
natural (d) unnecessary (a)	unkind (b) unhealthy (c)

7. Discussion.

What is your eating habit? Do you want a change?

① **Debate**. S: Eating meat is… Because…

② **Free talk**. What do you think of being a vegan?

Show the students a healthy eating habit—Food pyramid...

T: Food provides us with energy. Even meat is nutritious and helpful to our body.

Meat is an important part in our daily life. I think eating vegetables only is not a good choice. What do you think of being a vegan?

Ss: I think/ feel… / I don't think …

③ **Suggestion-making**. Let the students give some suggestions to the given eating habits.

④ The teacher guide the students to make a conclusion of being healthy.

It's wrong to eat meat.

Eating meat is…  vs. 

for		against	
unkind	(b)		
unnecessary	(a)	natural	(d)
unhealthy	(c)		

Food Guide Pyramid

The Five Food Groups are the building blocks of the Food Guide Pyramid.

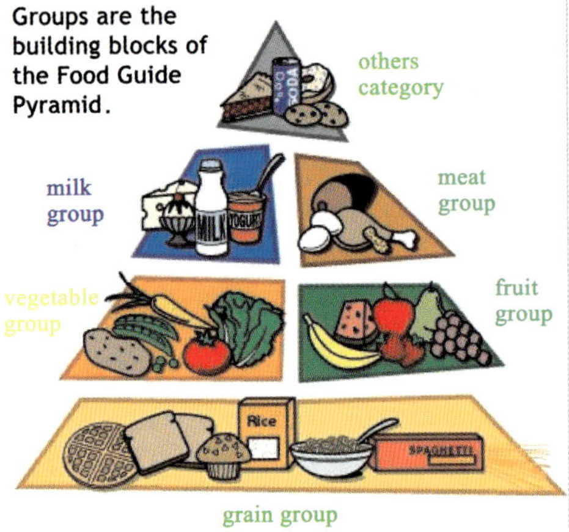

◆What do you think of being a vegan?

I think ...

I feel ...

I don' t think...

I agree/disagree...

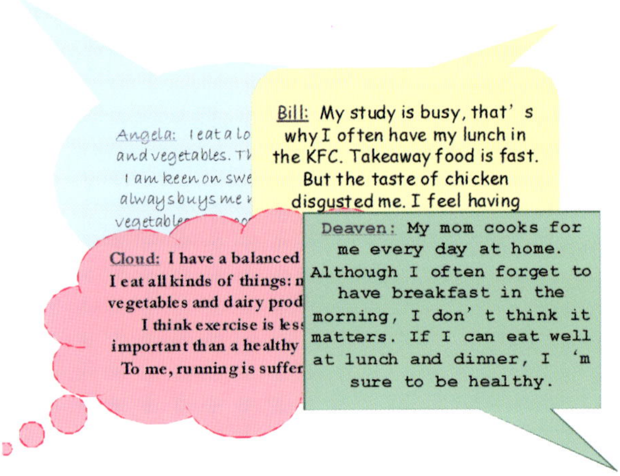

The secret of being healthy:

- a balanced diet
- exercise
- regular life
- good mood

Evaluate

评估教学活动的实际效果，分析学习成效，帮助学生排除学习障碍。

8. Homework: ① Recite the passage.
②Write about your current eating habit.

Evaluation ways include responses from teachers, other students and themselves. The students are encouraged to express their options about food freely, and also they should learn to understand different choices and opinions.

For the students of different levels, they can learn something form different parts of the lesson, all of them have the chance to say something about the topic, more or less.

More help will be given after class or in the next class in forms of exercise or homework. The teacher will know what problems the students may have in learning.

Notes:

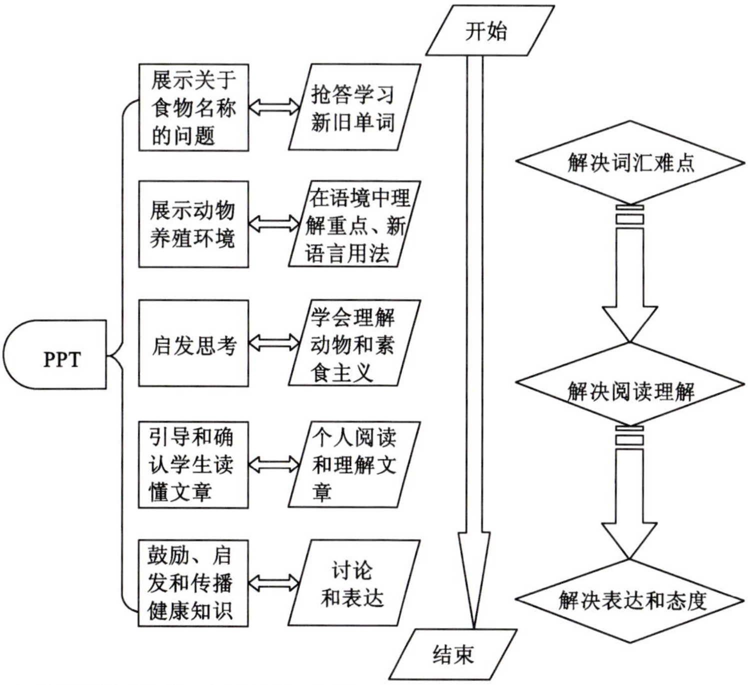

课程设计及反思

教师：徐佳

本课选取上海外语教育出版社和朗文出版的《展望未来》系列教材学生用书第二册第8单元 Cooking a Meal 的第二部分的阅读文章 The Food We Eat。

本课以阅读为基础训练学生的思辨能力，教育学生理解不同的选择，推广健康的饮食态度。在语言知识方面，重点是描述食品及其特点的形容词以及表达看法和对争论做出反应的句型。采用任务和交际教学法以及 ABCDE 五步教学模式设计课堂。

在激活环节中用禽畜动物的图片引发学生对肉制品的联想，复习词汇，练习描述食品特点的形容词，然后迅速进入下一个构建环节，延续前一个话题，再列出生活中少见的肉类，例如狗肉、兔肉、驴肉等，这些少数人吃过的肉类会使大部分学生产生一种难以接受的感觉，由此提出单词 disgusting，这是本课的重要词汇。接着，让学生思考动物的感受，给学生看一些动物被喂养和被宰杀的不人性照片，在此过程中引出本课其他几个重要词汇及其基本用法(in bad conditions，suffer)。至此，重难点基本构建完毕。

在养成环节中，直接转入课文内容，介绍正是由于看到上述情况，一部分人选择吃素(vegetarian)，更有少数人连奶蛋类食品都不吃，成为严格的素食主义者(vegan)。通过扫读，让学生说出两个主角饮食习惯的区别，通过通读，让学生关注细节，完成一系列的阅读练习。至此，对于课文出现的重难点在情景中的应用学生已经很熟悉了。

在发展和评估环节中，从教材第61页第六个连线题开始和学生进行一系列的讨论和辩论活动。在这个步骤中，学生以小组为单位活动，他们是发言的主角，教师的作用是引导学生多用、善用本课学的句型和词汇，并启发其对观点的提炼。学生发言的平台包括表达对素食的看法，对不同的观点进行驳斥，对不正确的饮食习惯提出建议等。在这个过程中，全班同学和教师都会对发言者进行评价，教师侧重于综合和提炼观点，把握气氛和进度，并纠正语言错误。

本课环节完整，节奏感强，发展部分自然，发言面广，训练到位。不足之处在于时间有点紧，需要学生高度配合。但由于这一课的授课对象是初三临近毕业、成绩差不多的一部分学生，所以达到了预期效果。也可根据学生情况删减“对他人的饮食习惯提建议”这样的环节。

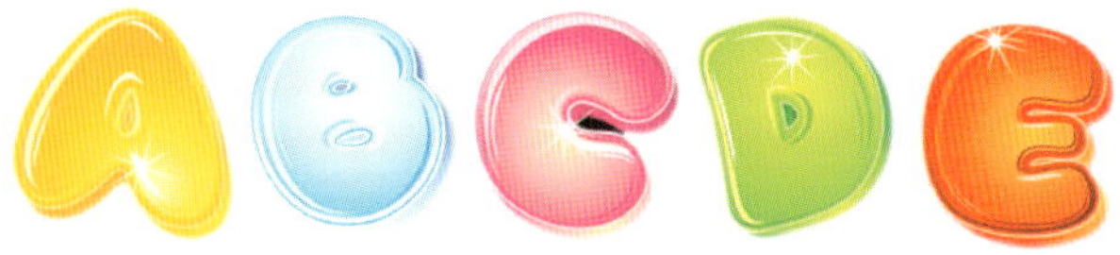

情景教学法

英语情景教学法

李思思

著名教育家陶行知先生说：“教学艺术就在于设法引起学生的兴味，有了兴味就肯用全副的精力去做事情。”情景教学法就是一种促使教学过程变成永远能引起学生极大的兴趣，能激发学生向知识领域不断探索的教育方法。正如布鲁姆所说：“成功的外语课堂教学应当在课内创设更多的情景，让学生有机会运用已学到的语言材料。”在英语教学过程中，教师要充分创设情景调动学生的思维，让学生学会探索，学会学习，学会运用英语。

情景教学法是指在教学过程中，教师有目的地引入或创设具有一定情绪色彩的、以形象为主体的生动具体的场景，以引起学生一定的态度体验，从而帮助学生理解教材，并使学生的心理机能得到发展的教学方法。情景教学法的核心在于激发学生的情感。情景教学是在对社会和生活进一步提炼和加工后才影响学生的。诸如榜样作用、生动形象的语言描绘、课内游戏、角色扮演、诗歌朗诵、绘画、体操、音乐欣赏、旅游观光，等等，都是寓教学内容于具体形象的情景之中，其中也就必然存在着潜移默化的暗示作用。英语情景教学就是以情景教学基本理论为基础，通过铺设情景，实现达到语言交际的目标。

英语情景教学法，是指教师根据学生的年龄特点和心理特征，遵循反映论的认知规律，结合教学内容，充分利用形象，创设具体生动的情景，使抽象的语言形式变成生动具体的可视语言，创设尽可能多的英语语言环境，让学生更多地接触和感受英语、说英语，用英语进行思维，用英语的方式主导行为。在英语教学中，教师创设真实的语言环境或模拟情景，充分利用生动、形象、逼真的意境，使学生产生身临其境的感觉，利用情景中传递的信息和语言材料，激发学生用英语表达思想感情的欲望，从而培养学生运用英语理解和表达的能力，激发学生从整体上理解和运用语言，促进学生的语言能力及情感、意志、想象力、创造力等的整体发展。该教学法的特点：将言、行、情景融为一体，有较强的直观性、科学性和趣味性。

情景教学法自 20 世纪 70 年代形成以来，已逐渐发展成为语言教学中一种基本的思想和教学方向。情景教学法的语言理论基础是英国的结构主义语言理论。口语被认为是语言的基础，结构是说话能力的核心。与美国结构主义语言学不同的是，在这里语言被看做是与现实世界的目标和情景有关的有目的的活动。这些活动是有交际意义的。教学要为用语言进行有效实践创造条件，要把学习手段与其最终的交际目的紧密结合起来。英语教学的过程就是语言交际能力的习得过程，学生在交际中不断地掌握语言技能、语言知识和语言特点。

情景教学法的理论依据主要有三点：第一，学生的心理和年龄特点。学生，尤其是中小学学生，有强烈的求知欲，爱幻想，思维有明显的具体形象性特征，情景教学可使学生充分发挥想象力和创造力。第二，语言的习得规律。语言的习得不是从词汇与语法规则入手的，语言是在语境中学习，在应用中掌握的。第三，学生的学习规律。情景教学可充分调动学生有意识的心理活动，充分挖掘学生无意识的心理活动。使学生在轻松愉快的气氛中，进行积极的、有创造性的学习，使整个身心得到和谐发展。

情景可以使学生产生言语的动机，并提供言语的材料，促进其语言运用能力的发展。在中学英语课堂教学中，教师应善于利用各种方式，巧妙运用各种教学媒体和手段创设教学情景，多方面调动学生的感官，让学生多渠道地获得信息，让学生用心去体验学习的内容，让学生在情景中去交流、发展，从而使学生较快地掌握所学的知识。创设情景的方法很多，我搜集并整理了我校一些成功的教学经验材料，总结如下：

一、利用实物，巧设情景

心理学研究证明，学习者对提供的教学形象能迅速感知，提高教学效率。但识别同一内容用不同的方式具有不同的识别速度。

用语言介绍，识别时间为2.8秒。

用线条图表介绍，识别时间为1.5秒。

用黑白照片介绍，识别时间为0.9秒。

展示实物，识别时间为0.4秒。

由此可见，教学所展示的形象越是鲜明，越是具体，就越能缩短感知时间，激发学生认知的兴趣，提高教学效率。

初中阶段有很多单词是表示具体事物的，所以教师在教有关单词的时候，可以用实物或者实物模型来呈现，利用实物教学很容易引起学生的兴趣。在 Unit 9 Food and Drink 这节课的 Lead in 环节中，我通过展示各种食物的实物、教具和一些 PPT，直观地展现了一些有关食物的图片。这样做的目的是使学生获得某一事物的外在感官认识。不仅能为学生学习新知识提供丰富的感性材料，而且能激发学生学习的兴趣，提高学习的效率。而一些常见的句型也可以通过视听方式来呈现，而不需要做过多的语法解释和句意翻译。

二、语言描述，引入情景

教学中，教师可以运用简单易懂的话语，做绘声绘色的描述，引导学生进入情景。例如教师可以一边播放幻灯片，一边播放音乐，然后描述。何盼老师在 Unit 9 Food and Drink 这节课的句型教学中，创设了一个和学生聊天的情景，在学生已有的知识背景下和学生以快餐为话题聊天，在聊天的过程中引出新句型。她还为学生设计了一个当快餐店小经理的游戏，让他们在介绍自己快餐店的真实情景中熟练地掌握这些句型。

三、利用动作、表情等体态语展现情景

在交际活动中，体态语起到了举足轻重的作用。体态语有很强的暗示作用，有利于组织教学：体态语具有直观性，便于学生理解；具有趣味性，能激发学生的兴趣。英语教师

在课堂上要积极运用各种生动传神的表情、形象的语言和演示动作来描述事实，力求逼真，以帮助学生理解并且逐步培养学生用英语进行思维的能力。例如在教 smile 一词时，教师可以做一个微笑的表情，在教 laugh 一词时，可以做一个大笑的表情，诸如此类。

四、利用多媒体教学手段，模拟创设情景

在英语教学中，应该始终坚持视听说领先的原则。樊娲老师在 Warming up 的环节中，通过 PPT 展示不同的局部图片让学生充分发挥想象力，猜想这些图片中人物的职业，目的是让学生明白，不同的职业有不同的穿衣要求和风格。因为是以游戏的形式出现的，学生很感兴趣，在不断地猜测过程中，学生由开始的漫无目的的瞎猜变成不知不觉地开始从服饰来猜测。因此，在课堂上，运用录像、投影和录音机为学生创造了一种悦目、悦耳、悦心的英语交际情景，形象生动，图文并茂。学生怀着轻松愉快的心情，边看边听，积极参与对话，充分发挥自己的想象力，进行语言交际活动并在情景中产生交流的真实感。

五、利用表演，体会情景

英语课堂教学中的表演可以分为机械性和发展性两种。前者指学生就课文内容进行表演，如分角色朗读、表演，这样的活动使教学情景真切地再现在学生面前，学生迅速感知教材内容，并能很容易地理解教材内容。故事中的“事”好像是自己做的，故事中的“话”好像是自己说的。扮演得越逼真就越感到亲切，越感到愉快，越感到学习的轻松。教师有时候也可以扮演一些角色，让学生更好地融入课堂气氛中去。在 Unit 9 Food and Drink 这课中，我在 Warming up 环节中，扮演了一个 waitress，预设了一个情景，与学生练习点餐的基本对话，让学生和教师迅速地进入状态。

发展性表演是指在所学课文内容的基础上，结合课文中有关日常生活的内容，利用所学句型进行带创造性的表演，引导学生进入“生活”，让学生自己创造情景，积极思维，丰富想象。在运用语言的过程中，巩固所学的知识，培养他们的能力。如在学完 Food and Drink 这一课，教师设计了让学生自己去餐厅聚会的情景，然后点餐。这是每个学生已经拥有的生活经验，在表演中，学生用学过的句型和自身的经验，创造性地灵活运用语言规律，充分调动了学生的积极性，培养了他们即兴发言的思维能力。另外樊娲老师在 Development 环节中也给学生创设了三种情景，要求学生通过小组讨论和合作完成小品演出。这一部分是学生最感兴趣的部分。因为这一部分采用了表演的方式，充分调动了学生的积极性。学生能够运用自己所学的知识模拟真实情景。同时，所提供的三个情景也充满了戏剧色彩，学生在情景中锻炼了灵活运用语言知识的能力和表演能力。

六、课外创设情景

除了在课堂上运用情景教学法，教师应该引导学生自主地创设环境，因为课堂时间毕竟有限，课堂上教师为学生所创设的景物、场景也是有限的。我们可以布置教室以创设英语学习的环境或是在课桌、墙上贴上单词和句子，让学生受到更多的英语熏陶。还有就是

可以充分利用教师的宣传栏、黑板报，让学生在黑板上轮流写出自己收集到的“英语新发现”。教师甚至可以为学生集体录制一些有关于英语的新信息及有价值的资料，让学生充分感受到学习英语的氛围。

总之，情景教学法是提高英语教学效果行之有效的好方法。它把简单刻板的教与学融合到多姿多彩的真情实境中，拆去了传统教与学的樊篱，让师生和谐地融为一体，在欢乐、活跃的氛围中激发学生的学习激情，培养学生的学习兴趣，化抽象为直观，化刻板为生动，帮助学生寻找到掌握英语的捷径，使学生学于其中，乐于其中，感于其中，从而提高教学质量。

Teaching Plan of *An Intergrated English Course*
Book 2 Unit 4 Clothing Item 1

教师：樊娲

Teaching Aims:

1. Learn some words about different kinds of clothing and the colors and styles of clothing.
2. Learn to comment on clothing.
3. Know that people should wear different clothes on different occasions.

Teaching Objects:

Junior 2.

Language Points:

1. Some words on clothing.
2. How to talk about clothing.
3. How to wear suitable clothes.

Teaching Aids:

Multi-media, tape-recorder.

Teaching Methods:

Task-based Language Teaching Approach.

Teaching Procedures	
Activate 在课堂教学开始前的较短时间内灵活安排新颖的导入活动，促使全班学生集中注意力，迅速进入学习状态。	**1. Let the Ss play a guessing game. Show the Ss some pictures of parts of the clothes and let the Ss guess the jobs of different people according to their clothes.** **Jobs: model, air-hostess, mechanic, waiter and waitress, nurse, doctors ...**  **2. Ask the Ss how they know their jobs.** **3. Comment: people doing different jobs should wear different clothes.**

Build

运用综合教学方法指导教学设计，营造良好的学习氛围，使学生快乐、自然、轻松、有效地学习语言。

1. Review the new words on clothing and give them some supplementary words.

Clothes: coat, vest, shirt, sweater, rain-jacket, suit, tie, bow-tie, pajamas, skirt…

Shoes: sneakers, sandals, slippers, leather shoes, sports shoes…

2. Learn the different styles of clothes.

Compare: casual and formal, classic and fashionable.

style

classic　　fashionable

3. **Learn the different colors: dark colors and vivid colors.**

colour

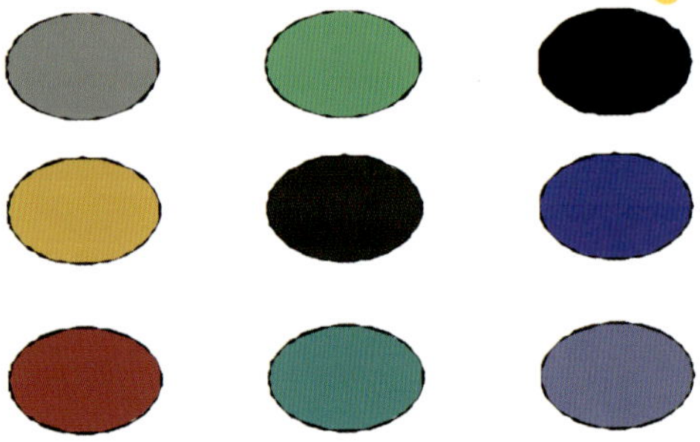

dark colours

colour

vivid colours

4. Free-talk.

Ask the Ss to talk in groups about their favourite clothes, styles and colors. And ask the Ss why they like them.

What kind of clothing do you like best?
Which style do you like best?
What colour do you like best?
Why?

*C*ultivate

按照启发式教学原则，设计饶有趣味的训练来充分调动学生学习的主动性。

1. Listen and grasp the main idea.

2. Listen and do Ex. 1 on the Ss' Book.

Listen to Item 1 and fill in the blanks.

1. Whitney likes __fun__ clothes.
2. Whitney's mother wears more __classic__ clothes.
3. Whitney thinks __young__ __girls__ should have more vivid colours.
4. David wears informal clothes like __jeans__ and __T-shirts__.
5. David thinks smart girls are usually more interested in __music__, __sports__, or __movies__.

3. Read after the tape.

4. Talk about the different ideas of the two people in the Ss' Book.

Develop

设计真实的语言环境来综合概括构建及养成部分所传达的语言信息，巩固课堂教学、衔接新旧知识、贯通前后内容，帮助学生学习训练，复习巩固。

1. Describe the clothes.

Give the Ss some pictures of different kinds of clothing and ask them to talk in groups and try to describe the pictures.

2. Act it out.

Give the Ss some interesting situations and ask them to use their imagination and act the scenes out.

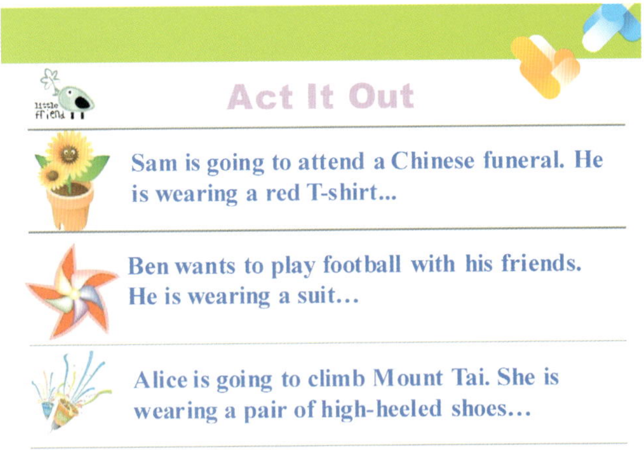

3. Comment: People should wear different kinds of clothes on different occasions.

1. Discussion

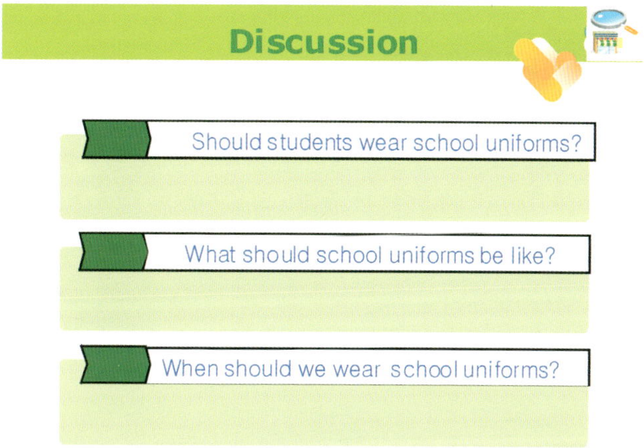

*E*valuate

评估教学活动的实际效果，分析学习成效，帮助学生排除学习障碍。

2. Homework

① Ask the Ss to write about his /her own ideas on school uniforms.

② Recite Item 1.

③ Ask the Ss to design a school uniform for our school.

3. Teaching Reflection

① The guessing game can attract the students' attention so that they can be more concentrated in the class. The teacher should provide some pictures for them and teach them some supplementary words on clothing.

② This unit is about clothing which is a very popular topic among the youth. The teacher should stimulate the students' interests about clothing by playing games and showing them some beautiful pictures. So the student find that this topic is interesting and easy to talk about.

③ At the end of the class, the students can use what they have just learnt to talk about different kinds of clothes. They know that different people should wear different clothes on different occasions. And they can try to design their ideal school uniforms.

④ The students can have more time to search more information on the Internet after class.

课程设计及反思

教师：樊娲

我选取的教材文本是“全国外国语学校系列教材”《英语综合教程》初中一年级第二学期第四单元的 Item 1。本课是一节听说课。

这节课的教学目的：1. 使学生掌握关于服饰种类、服饰风格和颜色的词汇。2. 学会谈论着装。3. 了解着装应符合职业和场合的需要。为了更好地完成教学目的，我使用了任务型教学法。

具体步骤如下所示。

第一步：Activate 激活

这个环节采取的是自然教学法。在这项活动中，我通过展示不同的局部图片让学生充分发挥想象力，猜想该图片中人物的职业，目的是让学生明白，不同的职业有不同的穿衣要求和风格。因为是以游戏的形式进行教学的，学生很感兴趣，在不断地猜测过程中，学生由开始的漫无目的的瞎猜变成不知不觉地从服饰来猜测。

第二步：Build 构建

这一环节分为两个部分。第一部分采用直接教学法，通过展示图片并用英语直接进行教学，学生在这个步骤中学习大量有关服饰的词汇，同时扩展到服饰的颜色和风格范畴。

第二部分采取沟通式教学法，学生通过在上一步骤所获知的知识，运用信息互补(Information Gap)、自由选择(Choice)、回馈(Feedback)等方式，达到真正沟通的目的。这一部分要求学生分组谈论自己最喜欢的服饰、颜色和风格，以及做此选择的原因。

学生在这一环节中，因为在短时间内接触到大量的信息，部分学生可能无法立刻吸收，因此有些学生在 free-talk 阶段感觉有些困难。因此，该部分的教学可以加大练习量，使学生更加快速和准确地掌握基本词汇，并灵活运用。

第三步：Cultivate 养成

这一环节为课文文本教学，采用了任务型教学法，通过一个个任务完成教学。首先，学生听课文并掌握大意。接着，要求学生在掌握大意的前提下填空。然后要求学生跟读并纠正发音，这一部分采用了听说教学法。最后要求学生总结课文中二人的不同穿衣理念。

第四步：Develop 发展

这一环节采用的也是任务型教学法。第一步，给学生展示了八幅不同的图片，要求学生模仿本课课文，运用关键句型谈论图片中人物的着装。这一部分的任务设置由浅入深，学生在学习中水到渠成地完成了所有的步骤。虽然最后部分学生感觉有难度，但都能在基本句型的指引下完成任务。

第二步，给学生创设了三种情境，要求学生通过小组讨论和合作完成小品的演出。这一部分是学生最感兴趣的部分。因为这一部分采用了表演的方式，充分调动了学生的积极性。学生能够运用自己所学的知识模拟真实情景。同时，所提供的三个情境也是充满戏剧色彩的，学生在情境中锻炼了灵活运用语言知识的能力和表演能力。因此，也可以说这一部分是情境教学法的充分运用。

第五步：Evaluate 评价

这一环节分为两个部分。第一部分为任务型教学法。在这一部分给学生创设一个真实的情境，刚好学校近期在制作校服，要求学生根据提示完成讨论：学生应不应该穿校服？校服应该设计成什么样子？学生如果有校服应该什么时候穿着？

第二部分为课后内容，即家庭作业，要求学生在课后对刚才的讨论进行总结，写一篇 80 字左右的文章，另外要求学生在课后设计一套自己喜欢的校服。

综上所述，本课在任务型教学法的大前提指引下，在不同的步骤又采取了不同的教学法。学生通过独立思考、回顾学习、讨论合作完成不同的任务，从而完成学习。当然，教学的具体步骤中也有一些不足之处值得思考，如在课文听说训练中如何提高学生的兴趣？有些步骤是否可以有更好的处理方式？我认为这些都值得在日常教学中不断反思并总结修改。

Teaching Plan of *An Integrated English Course* Book 1 Unit 9 Food and Drink Getting Started and Dialogue 2

教师：李思思

Teaching Aims:

1. Knowledge aims: to get the students to master some new words about food and drink.
2. Ability aims: to enable the students to make an order in a restaurant and master some useful sentences.
3. Emotional aims: to get the students to know how to make a party in a restaurant and share with their friends.

Teaching Objects:

Junior One.

Language Points:

Words: steak, chip, bean, sprite, hamburger, rare, medium, well-done

Sentences: Would you like to order?
What would you like to…?
Would you like something to …?
I'd like to …

Teaching Aids:

The multi-media equipments, the tape-recorder, handouts, some food and drink as gifts.

Teaching Methods:

1. Situational Teaching Method.
2. Communicative Approach.

Teaching Procedures

Activate

在课堂教学开始前的较短时间内灵活安排新颖的导入活动，促使全班学生集中注意力，迅速进入学习状态。

Step 1 Greetings and Duty Show

Step 2 Warming-up

Today, I prepare some food for you. I bought some food from our dinning-room.

T: Tony, what would you like to have?

S: I'd like to have a sandwich.

T: Congratulations. It's for free. Here you are.

T: Yuri, what would you like to have?

S: I'd like ...

T: No food left now. I feel tired and hungry. Can you help me?

S: What would you like to have? Would you like something to eat?

T: I'm full. I'm not very hungry. But I am thirsty now. Can you help me?

S: What would you like to drink?

T: I'd like a bottle of cola.

S: Sorry. I haven't got a bottle of cola. But I have a bottle of sprite.

T: It's very kind of you. Thank you very much. I am not thirsty and hungry now. You've done a very good job today.

Use some pictures of food to practice the sentences.

<table>
<tr><td></td><td>

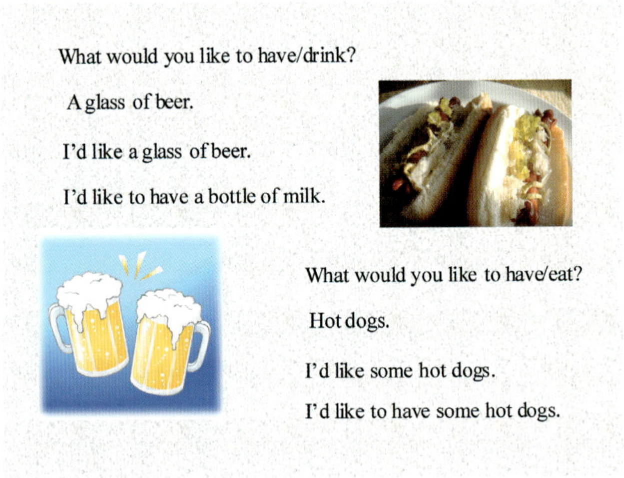

What would you like to …?
I'd like to …
</td></tr>
<tr><td></td><td>
Step 3　Lead-in
T：Now, we don't have any food. Where shall we go now?
Don't worry. Let's go to a restaurant. (Show a picture of a restaurant.)
</td></tr>
</table>

*B*uild

运用综合教学方法指导教学设计，营造良好的学习氛围，使学生快乐、自然、轻松、有效地学习语言。

Restaurant

T：When we go to a restaurant, who will serve us? Who will give us some water to drink?

S：Waiter or waitress.

T：Now we are going to a restaurant. Watch video, and tell me what they are doing.

T：What are they reading?

S：They are reading a **menu**.

MAYFLOWER RESTAURANT

MENU

STARTERS

Soup……………….$2.95

…………………………

MAIN COURSES

Steak……………….$13.00

…………………………

DESSERT

Salad……………….$3.25

…………………………

DRINKS

Water……………….$1.50

…………………………

T：And watch another one. What are they doing?

S：They are ordering. They are asking for food and drink.

Step 4 Guessing Game

What can we make from the food?

Tomato paste, bread, sausage.

We can make a hot dog.

…

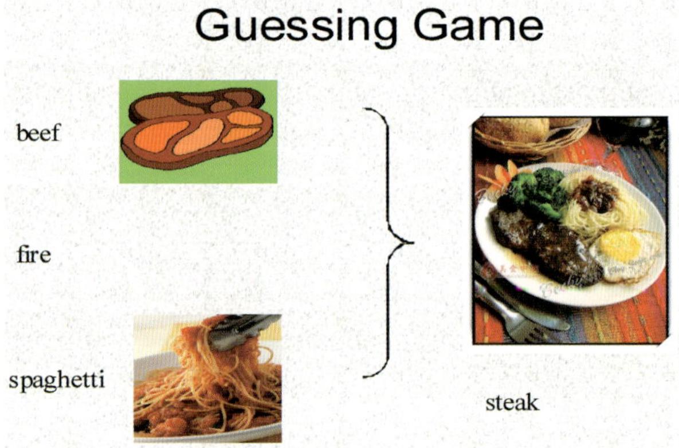

*C*ultivate

按照启发式教学原则，设计饶有趣味的训练来充分调动学生学习的主动性。

Step 5　Teaching Procedure

1. Listen and answer.

Dialogue 2

Questions to answer:

1. ***Where are they?***
2. ***Does the man want any beef?***
3. ***How does he like it?***
4. ***What salad does he like?***
5. ***What does the man drink?***

2. Listen and read.

Develop

设计真实的语言环境来综合概括构建及养成部分所传达的语言信息，巩固课堂教学、衔接新旧知识、贯通前后内容，帮助学生学习训练，复习巩固。

Step 6　Development：Group Work

Please make a dialogue when you eat in a restaurant.

You can use these sentences：

Group Work:

Please have a big dinner with your classmates.

You can use these sentences:

For waiter: Can I help you?

What would you like to eat/drink?

Would you like something to eat/drink?

Would you like to order, please?

For diner: I'd like a/some…

I'd like to have a/some…

<table>
<tr><td></td><td>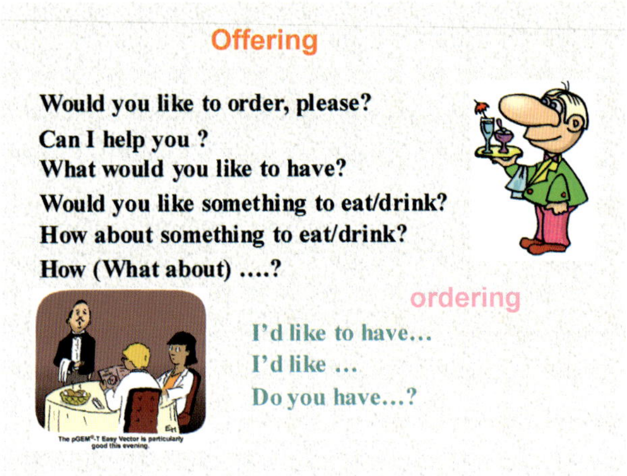
</td></tr>
<tr><td>Evaluate

评估教学活动的实际效果，分析学习成效，帮助学生排除学习障碍。</td><td>Step 7　Homework

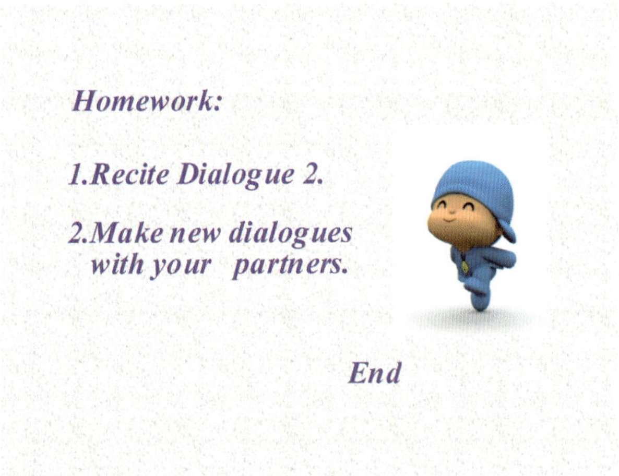

Teaching Reflection
The teacher made good use of 45 minutes to get the students to practise their listening, speaking, reading and writing. And all the teaching aims are achieved.</td></tr>
</table>

课程设计及反思

教师：李思思

我选取的教材文本是“全国外国语学校系列教材”《英语综合教程》初中一年级第一学期第九单元 Food and Drink 中 Getting Started and Dialogue 2，是一节听说课。

我这节课的教学目的如下：

1. 使学生能听、说、读一些关于食物的单词。如 steak，chip，bean，sprite，hamburger，rare，medium，well-down 等并了解其含义。

2. 使学生能灵活运用重点句型，并清楚其运用的场合和语气。

Would you like to order?

What would you like to ...?

Would you like something to ...?

I'd like to ...

3. 使学生能模仿课文对话，并在一定的语境中运用所学的语言知识进行交际。

我主要使用了以下教学法：情景教学法和听说法。

具体步骤如下：

第一步：Activate 激活

在这个环节中，教师扮演了一位 waitress，预设了一个情景，与学生练习点餐时的基本对话。

第二步：Build 构建

在 Lead-in 环节中，使用了演示法，通过展示各种食物、教具和 PPT，直观地展现了一些有关食物的图片。这样做的目的是使学生获得某一事物的外在感官认识。演示法不仅能为学生学习新知识提供丰富的感性材料，而且能激发学生学习的兴趣，提高学习的效果。

第三步：Cultivate 养成

在讲解 Dialogue 2 时使用了听说法。

1. 认知，即对所学句型耳听意会。通过对比英语与汉语的相同点或不同点，使学生从对比中了解新句型。

2. 模仿，即跟读、齐读、抽读，纠错并改正；同时记忆。

3. 重复和检查，学生重复模仿材料，做各种记忆性练习；同时教师要进行检查。当确信学生已能正确理解、朗诵所学句型之后，才能进行下一步的变换活动。

4. 变换，即替换操练，应按替换、转换、扩展三步逐渐加大难度。同时要注意学生的理解情况。

5. 活用所学语言材料于交际实际或模拟情景之中，即综合运用。

第四步：Develop 发展

在 Development 中使用情景教学法，给学生预设了多个去餐厅的情景，如去必胜客餐厅参加同学聚会，去肯德基过生日，去西餐厅家庭聚餐，等等，让学生通过这些情景练习已学会的句型。

第五步：Evaluate 评价

这一环节分为两个部分。第一部分给学生创设一个真实的情境，让学生自由发挥，创作在餐厅的对话。第二部分为课后内容，即家庭作业，要求学生在课后背诵课文并继续完成对话练习。

综上所述，关于教学方法的概念，人们给过很多不同的解释。如有人认为："教学方法是教师为了完成教学任务，实现教学目的，在教学过程中所采用的一系列方法和措施。"也有人认为："教学方法是教师和学生为了完成教学任务、实现教学目的所采用的工作方式或手段。"我觉得这些解释不能充分解释教学方法的本质。"教学有法，教无定法。"我认为不同的教学目的和教学任务就需要采用不同的教学方法去实现和完成。

一般来说，我选择教学法的依据主要是以下几点。

依据教材内容的特点和课的类型：如果这节课是听说课，偏重口语练习，那么我会更多地使用情景教学法。

依据学生的实际情况：教师的教是为了学生的学，教学方法也要适应学生的基础条件和个性特征。选择丰富多彩的教具，使用简单的演示法更切合初一年级学生的实际水平。

依据教师本身的素养条件：有的方法虽然很好，但是如果教师自己驾驭不了，也不能在教学活动中产生良好的效果。所以我选择的这几种教学法都是平时常用的，也是自己比较熟悉的。当然今后我也会尝试更丰富的教学法。

Teaching Plan for *IE Book* Unit 9 Item 1

教师：何盼

Teaching Aims:

1. To get the students to know some new words and expressions about fast food and fast food restaurants.
2. To let them use the new words and expressions to describe fast food restaurants and express their own opinions.
3. To get the students to discuss advantages and disadvantages of fast food and keep a healthy diet.

Teaching Objects:

Junior One.

Language Points:

all over the world, service, industry, provide somebody (with) something

Teaching Aids:

PPT.

Teaching Methods:

1. Audio-visual Method.
2. Communicative Approach.
3. Situational Teaching Method.

<table>
<tr><th colspan="2">Teaching Procedures</th></tr>
<tr>
<td>

Activate

在课堂教学开始前的较短时间内灵活安排新颖的导入活动，促使全班学生集中注意力，迅速进入学习状态。

</td>
<td>

A Game

Ask a volunteer to stand in front of the students. The students can ask him/her questions begin with “what”, but the only answer to every question can be sausage. The first student who makes him/her laugh wins a try in the front.

</td>
</tr>
<tr>
<td>

Build

运用综合教学方法指导教学设计，营造良好的学习氛围，使学生快乐、自然、轻松、有效地学习语言。

</td>
<td>

Watch some pictures of fast food and fast food restaurants, lead in “adults” and “teenagers”, and tell why they like fast food restaurants, then lead in “service” and “provide”.

Ask the students to be the manager of my restaurant, they are going to introduce my restaurant to both adults and teenagers.

</td>
</tr>
</table>

	   Introduce some tradition in China and Western countries. Western people eat quietly. They do not share the same dish or plate. Chinese like to sit around a table to show friendship. Share food in the same plate. And talk and tell jokes loudly.

<table>
<tr>
<td></td>
<td>

</td>
</tr>
<tr>
<td>
Cultivate

按照启发式教学原则，设计饶有趣味的训练来充分调动学生学习的主动性。
</td>
<td>
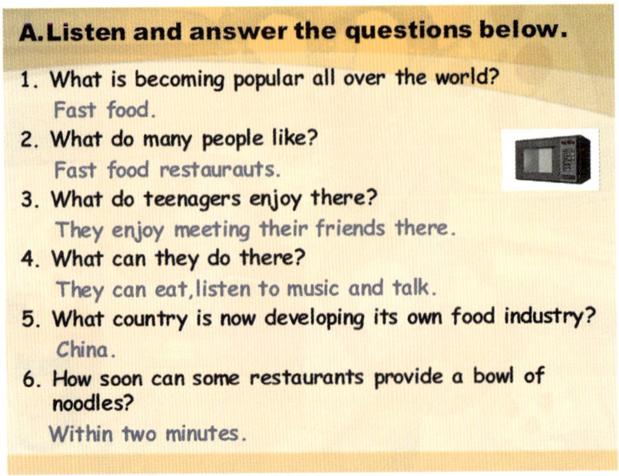

</td>
</tr>
</table>

B. Listen again and fill in the chart. (on page 158)

Fast food	is popular	all over the world
People	like	fast food restaurants
Teenagers	enjoy	meeting friends there
They	eat,listen to music and talk	________
Adults	like	these restaurants
China	is developing	its own fast food industry
Fast food	is part of life	for many people

C. Listen and read.

D. Listen and retell the passage with the help of the chart.

Fast food	is popular	all over the world
People	like	fast food restaurants
Teenagers	enjoy	meeting friends there
They	eat,listen to music and talk	________
Adults	like	these restaurants
China	is developing	its own fast food industry
Fast food	is part of life	for many people

<table>
<tr>
<td>

*D*evelop

设计真实的语言环境来综合概括构建及养成部分所传达的语言信息，巩固课堂教学、衔接新旧知识、贯通前后内容，帮助学生学习训练，复习巩固。

</td>
<td>

Watch a video and grab the main idea.

Then, divide the class into two teams, and debate “Is fast food good for us?”

</td>
</tr>
<tr>
<td>

*E*valuate

评估教学活动的实际效果，分析学习成效，帮助学生排除学习障碍。

</td>
<td>

Write down your own opinions about fast food and fast food restaurants.

</td>
</tr>
</table>

课程设计及反思

教师：何盼

本节课是一节新教师共同成长的展示课，教学对象是初一年级二班的学生。教学内容是《英语综合教程》第二册第九单元 Item 1，主要是让学生了解快餐店并学会用新词来描述快餐店的食物、服务等，这是一节情景教学法贯穿始终的展示课。

第一步：Activate 激活

通过一个“腊肠”小游戏吸引学生的注意力，让学生对食物产生兴趣。

第二步：Build 构建

在这一环节我遵循《教学大纲》的原则和“情景英语教学法”的要求，给出了一系列有关快餐的图片，让学生说出这些食物的名称，学生对这些好吃的食物十分感兴趣，全班同学都积极地参与进来。接着学生自己总结出这些食物都是快餐。我马上让学生在真实的情境中发挥，青少年和成年人都爱吃快餐，那么快餐厅里都提供些什么呢？之后我马上让学生用新句型 provide somebody with something 和前面说过的食物名称进行操练。在练习之后我还向学生介绍了一些西方国家和中国饮食习惯的不同之处，让学生感受外国的风土人情。与此同时也能使学生产生兴趣，十分愿意按小组进行口头练习。学生参与度很高，十分愿意向大家展示自己的英语口语。在整个构建的过程中，我结合了本课的生词和词组，学生在游戏和练习的过程中已经能够理解和熟练运用这些单词和词组了。

第三步：Cultivate 养成

这一环节是对构建环节的强化，需要教师按照启发式教学原则，设计饶有趣味的训练来充分调动学生学习的主动性，实现教师主导作用和学生主体作用的结合、系统知识学习与智力充分发展的结合、书本知识和直接经验的结合，帮助学生加强对新知识、新能力的掌握。在这一环节我分听课文、读课文、根据表格复述课文三个步骤让学生对课文有很好的理解。课文中的生词和词组都是学生前面已经学过并熟悉了的。由于生词和词组也在构建环节中得到学习，所以在复述环节中大部分学生能够比较顺利地将所学课文复述出来，也能很好地建立学生学习英语的信心和兴趣。

第四步：Develop 发展

在这一环节我通过一个英语辩论活动，让学生通过运用前面所学的知识表达对快餐店的看法。

第五步：Evaluate 评价

在这节课的最后我评价了学生的英语活动，纠正了学生在语言练习中容易犯的错误，复习了本节课的学习内容，最后布置了课后作业。

☞ 教学反思：

情景教学法以真实的情境组织教学，在情境的履行过程中，以参与、体验、互动、交流、合作的学习方式，充分发挥学习者自身的认知能力，调动他们已有的目的语资源，在真实情景中感知、认识、应用目的语，在“干”中学，在“用”中学。能通过有趣的课堂交际活动有效地激发学习者的学习动机，使他们主动参与学习。

整节课以真实的情境贯穿始终，学生在真实的英语情境中不知不觉地学习并掌握了这节课的新知识。活动既不重复，也不简单枯燥，由易到难，环环相扣，使学生获得完成任务后的兴奋感和成就感。

听说教学法

听说教学法

夏涓涓

一、听说教学法的定义

听说教学法(Audio-lingual Teaching Method)是一种强调通过反复句型结构操练培养口语听说能力的教学法。在英语教学过程中，听说教学法得到不断完善，形成了规范的五个阶段：

1. 认知(recognition)，即对所学句型耳听意会，主要对比英语与汉语的相同点或不同点，使学生从对比中学习和了解新句型或话语。

2. 模仿(imitation)，即跟读、齐读、抽读，纠错并改正；同时记忆。

3. 重复和检查(repetition and check)，即学生重复模仿材料，做各种记忆性练习；同时教师要进行检查。当确信学生已能正确理解、朗诵所学句型之后，才能进行下一阶段的变换活动。

4. 变换(variation)，即替换操练，应按替换、转换、扩展三步逐渐加大难度。同时要注意学生的理解情况。

5. 选择(selection)，活用所学语言材料于交际实际或模拟情景之中，也就是综合运用。

二、听说教学法产生的历史和背景

20 世纪 40 年代开始，结构语言学、心理语言学、控制论、行为主义心理学等相互渗透的学科得到发展，外语教学日益依赖现代技术，各国教学法家竞相实验新的教学法体系。这些给听说教学法的产生提供了理论基础。美国国防部邀请了一批语言学家和外语教学法专家，研究新的外语教学法。其中为首的学者是布龙菲尔德(Leonard Bloomfield, 1887-1949)。布氏系用行为主义心理学研究语言的结构主义语言学的创立者，又与直接法大师帕默有过学术交往，结果便制订了以结构主义语言学和操练性条件反射为基础的陆军口语法，又称布龙菲尔德教学法。试验取得成功并逐渐完善为听说教学法并传及全世界。听说教学法又叫结构法或句型法，《英语 900 句》(*English 900*)是听说教学法的典型教材。

对听说教学法影响最大的是美国外语教学法家弗斯(Charies C. Fries, 1887-1967)和拉多(R. Lado)。弗斯严格区别 method 和 approach 的概念。他认为 method 是指教学方式、方法和教学技巧，而 approach 则是指达到教学目的的途径、路子和理论。由此可见，听说教学法或口语教学法是一种目的在于掌握口语的教学法体系。听说教学法把语言结构分析的研究成果运用到外语教学中，使教材的编写和教学过程的安排具有科学的依据。这对提高外语教学的效果，加速外语教学的过程无疑是非常重要的贡献和进步。

三、听说教学法在外校外语教学中的应用

1. 听说教学法在外校外语教学常规中的应用

听说教学法一直是外语学习的有效方法之一，它完全遵循了语言学习的规律，强调了听说领先，强化了句型结构的学习在语言学习中的重要作用。外校的外语教学传统一直强调“听说领先”。用听来输入，用不停的模仿强化，用“说”来输出。这个看似“慢”的教学过程，却在不知不觉中为学生打下了坚实的语言基础。这也贯穿着听说法“重复、模仿”的重要原则。这种听说领先的教学传统，我们一直坚持了四十多年。这与传统的外语教学“始终把培养阅读能力放在首要位置，听、说、写、译只是放在第二位，没有明确提出培养学生的语言交流能力”完全不同。因此外校在外语人才的培养上，具有自己独特的特色。

第一，听说领先。听说是一切语言活动的基础，口语是第一位的，读写是在听说的基础上派生出来的。强调“听”的必要性。与其他学校教师用中文讲解不同，外校要求全英文教学，使学生完全处于英语的环境中，培养了良好的语感。而且在模仿过程中，强调学生必须先听，听了之后才能模仿。

第二，强调“模仿”和“重复”的重要性。要求跟读、齐读、抽读、纠错、改正；同时记忆。在每节英语课上，教师给学生大量的时间模仿(个人、小组、大组)，针对模仿，教师还往往设计一些小型比赛活跃课堂气氛。只有通过每节课大量的模仿，学生才能打下坚实的语言基础。

第三，所有学过的课文，学生必须在教师面前背诵，语音、语调达到了要求才能过关。这种严格的要求给学生的口语打下了良好的基础。

2. 听说教学法在外语课堂教学实例中的应用

①强化句型，注重听和模仿

武汉外校使用的教材之一是《看听学》，这部经典的教材本身就是听说教学法的代表教材。课程就是围绕着“听音模仿，句型练习”来设计的。冯文力老师在《看听学》Television Day 中重点突出句型结构的练习。在句型操练中句型难度由浅入深，层层递进。同时，冯老师还坚持了 listen and repeat，这是外校外语教学的经典环节，是听说的核心体现。

②注重变换，不拘泥于单一的句型操练

在对语言材料的学习中，要使学生灵活运用，必须注重变换。变换即替换操练，应按替换、转换、扩展三步逐渐加大难度。同时要注意学生的理解情况。如董颜华老师的这节课非常强调“听”的重要性，基本上所有的语言材料都是以听的形式呈现的。同时她也注重替换和转换，问题由国外的节日转换到中国的节日，使学生在操练的过程中学会用所学句型来表达自己熟悉的东西。

又如夏涓涓老师关于 Wimbledon 的一节课中，对听说材料难度进行分层设计：BBC news 对应简单的时间(较简单)→课文内容录音及相关问题(难度适中)→拓展内容的视频(难度较大)，使不同程度的学生都能在课堂上得到提高。

③在交际实际或模拟情景之中活用所学语言材料

如夏涓涓老师关于 Wimbledon 的一节课中，在介绍了 Wimbledon 这个世界级的网球比赛后，又在教学活动中模拟了真实场景(WCG，即世界电子竞技大赛)，同时兼顾了学生的兴趣，让学生用介绍 Wimbledon 的句型来介绍 WCG。

四、听说教学法的优点和不足

1. 听说教学法的优点

①重视句型教学。句型结构训练避免了语法翻译法繁琐的语法分析，是学生掌握外语的有效手段。熟练地掌握句型，有利于外语语言习惯和外语思维的养成。

②强调外语教学的实践性，即教语言本身，而不是教有关语言的知识。

③重视口语能力的培养，在口语句型结构的基础上再学习书面语。听说训练有利于培养学生的听力理解能力和学到比较自然的语音语调，使学生在学习外语的初级阶段，在有限的材料范围内就能流利地听说外语。

④广泛利用对比的方法，在对比母语与外语的句型结构特点的基础上找出难点，根据由易到难安排句型操练，有针对性地编写教材，有利于加强重点和难点句型的训练和掌握，有利于学生更有效地学习和掌握外语。

⑤有利于教师组织材料、扩展对话，给教师以充分的发挥空间。

2. 听说教学法的不足

①把语言看做是一系列刺激—反应的行为过程，忽视语言训练和运用的创造性。

②在句型操练中一般不指明语法规则，同时也忽视词汇和语义的分析，这就使得学生对语言体系没有一个清晰的概念。加上句型操练是一种机械性的重复和记忆，学生的语言创造力得不到充分的发挥。

③听说教学法过于重视训练语言的形式，脱离语言的意义和交际来机械地操练语言结构，学的语言很不自然，不利于培养学生应付自然的语言交际的能力，有些学生能把句型背得滚瓜烂熟，但在交际场合却不会运用，或用得不恰当，甚至出错。

④把听说材料本身当成了教学方法，而不是将它看成是实施教学目的的教学辅助工具。

⑤过多地、机械地模仿和操练句型使学习者感到枯燥无味，不利于提高学习者的兴趣。

⑥通常是由教师决定听说材料和教学进度，不利于调动学生的学习积极性。

Teaching Plan of《综合英语》第三册第三单元 Wimbledon

教师：夏涓涓

Teaching Aims:

1. To form the ability of getting the main information from sports news.
2. To practice the ways and expressions of introducing international sports events.

Teaching Objects:

Junior 2.

Language Points:

provide with, attention, considerable

How/What/When...?

Teaching Aids:

A tape-recorder, a projector, and a computer.

Teaching Methods:

1. Audio-lingual Method.
2. Situational Teaching Method.

Teaching Procedures

	Lead-in (Pre-activities) **Step 1** Listening practice. Play two pieces of news from BBC with the following questions: 1. Which two sports are mentioned in the news? 2. How important is Wimbledon?

Activate

在课堂教学开始前的较短时间内灵活安排新颖的导入活动，促使全班学生集中注意力，迅速进入学习状态。

Step 2 Let the students guess what kind of sports we will learn this time by giving them a few tips, the students get clearer and more detailed information about tennis in the hope of reaching the topic of Wimbledon. It is designed to arouse the students' motivation and attraction.

Build

运用综合教学方法指导教学设计，营造良好的学习氛围，使学生快乐、自然、轻松、有效地学习语言。

Presentation（Structural Activities）

Step 1 After learning a few words about Wimbledon, the students are required to ask questions about the first tennis championship with the questions "when, where, who, how many". Encourage the students to ask as many questions as possible.

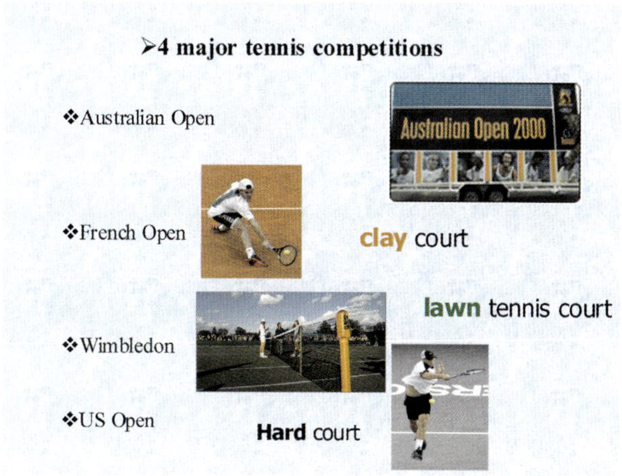

Step 2 By listening to the passage and repeating after each pause, the students can hopefully guess the meaning of the new words, if not, the teacher will assist in simple English when necessary.

Step 3 Listen to the tape and read after it sentence by sentence for further understanding. Then the teacher asks the students to introduce the Centre Courts with books shut.

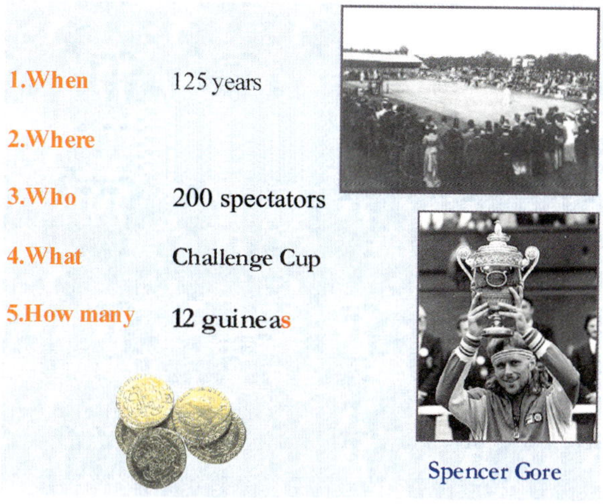

Ask the students to retell something about the Center Court with the help of the information in the PPT.

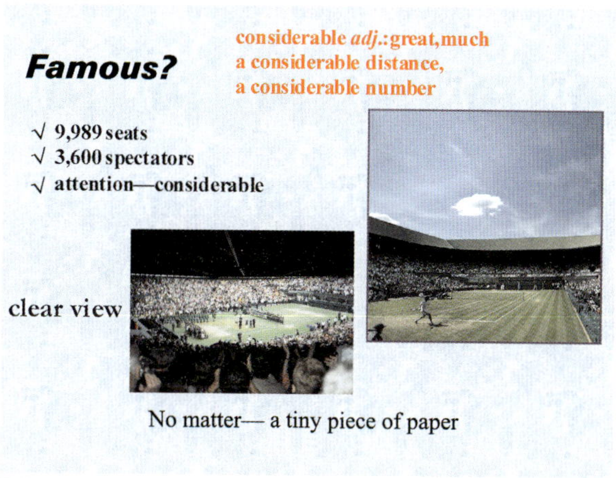

Step 4 Introduce Pete Samprus and the status of Wimbledon now.

Conclusion: How to introduce a sporting event?

Step 1 Guessing game.

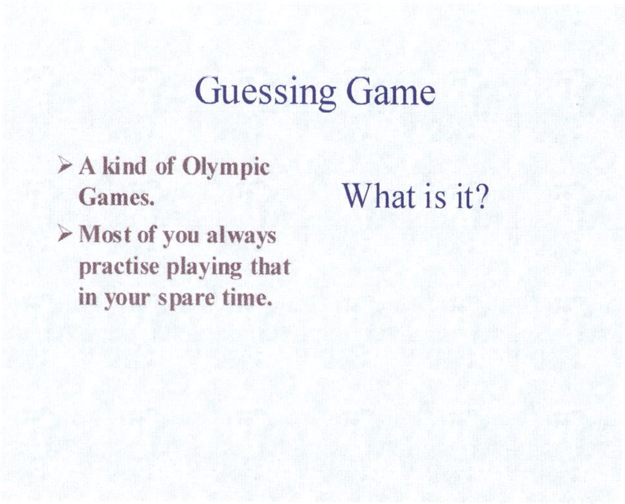

Step 2 Listening practice.

Ask some questions about WCG before the students watch the video.

What does WCG stand for?

When were the first Cyber Games held?

Step 3 Give the related information to the students and ask them to introduce WCG 2009.

*C*ultivate

按照启发式教学原则，设计饶有趣味的训练来充分调动学生学习的主动性。

<table>
<tr>
<td></td>
<td>
The History

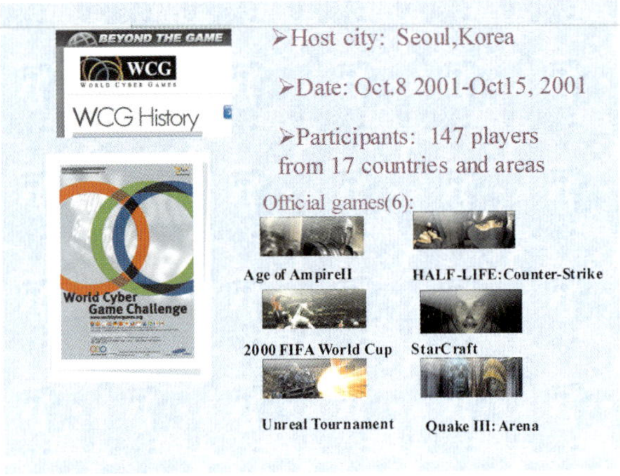

</td>
</tr>
<tr>
<td>
Develop

设计真实的语言环境来综合概括构建及养成的部分所传达的语言信息，巩固课堂教学、衔接新旧知识、贯通前后内容，帮助学生学习训练，复习巩固。
</td>
<td>
The Main Court

</td>
</tr>
</table>

The Hero

Activity

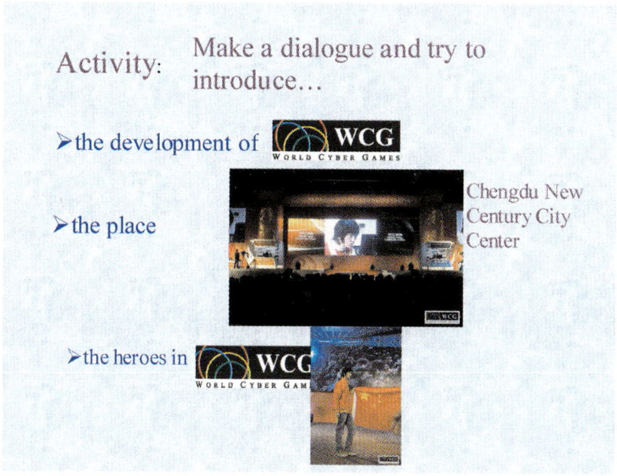

Ask the students to choose one of the three topics to introduce WCG.

*E*valuate 评估教学活动的实际效果，分析学习成效，帮助学生排除学习障碍。	The students are asked to introduce each part by using the sentence we have learnt today: Such as provide with... attention... considerable...

课程设计及反思

教师：夏涓涓

本课选取的教材文本是“全国外国语学校系列教材”《英语综合教程》初中二年级第一学期第六单元的 Item 1。本课是一节听说课。

这节课的教学目的：1．学会听新闻，特别是体育新闻，学会抓住新闻的几个要素。2．了解当今国际体育赛事，如网球的相关知识。3．学会用学到的表达方法来介绍当今体育赛事，如温布尔登网球公开赛。4．学会用本课学到的表达方法推而广之地介绍当今一些重要的有影响力的比赛。为了更好地达到教学目的，我综合使用了多种教学法。

具体步骤如下所示。

第一步：Activate 激活

本环节采用的是听说教学法。在这项活动中，我通过让学生听 BBC 新闻的形式来导入，引导学生听出新闻的几个要素，考虑到不同层面的学生，我特地把听力材料及问题的难度进行了调整，由浅入深，从而导入到要讲的主题温布尔登网球公开赛上来。

第二步：Build 构建

本环节分为三个部分。第一部分采用直接教学法和听说教学法，通过听材料进一步了解温网的相关知识，再通过图片帮助学生理解，学生在这个步骤中学习大量有关比赛的词汇和表达方法。再通过“听说复述的环节”让学生进一步强化和理解。

第二部分采用任务型教学法，学生通过上一步骤已经初步掌握了温网的相关知识以及介绍重大体育赛事的表达方法。设计一幅图片让学生对此进行复述，在这个过程中，学生可以选择自己掌握得较熟练的内容进行复述，在复述上进行大胆创新和适当运用合适连词的学生得到了最大程度的肯定和鼓励。

在这一环节中，由于时间短、知识容量和难度比较大，部分学生没有能力达到自由复述的要求，不过随着教师的鼓励和复述次数的增多，这个部分的任务能够很好地被完成。

第三部分是总结如何介绍一项赛事。其中有个让学生比较放松的拓展环节，介绍两大球星，这是课文细节的拓展（课文中介绍的是 Samprus，而学生对于 Ferderer 比较熟悉），通过比较，让学生更好地运用 serve 及 so that 的结构，还可以顺便让学生复习比较级。

在总结部分以关键词来引导学生：

如 history 引导学生用 when，place 引导学生用 where 等。这个部分强化了听说教学法中以句型结构为基础的教学方法。

第三步：Cultivate 养成

本环节在本课中是一个承上启下的环节，既检验了上一环节的课文内容，又为下一个环节的拓展做了铺垫。这一部分还是以听说法和视听法为主要教学方法。

教师播放一段关于 WCG(世界电子大赛)的视频介绍，问题正是承接第二步最后总结环节的内容，如 history, the place 等，所以虽然难度比较大，但由于学生已经熟悉相关内容，而且播放次数较多，学生还是能够迅速回答相关问题。这个环节运用的是听说教学法，要求学生集中注意力对信息进行记录和整合。

然后让学生对所记录的内容进行对比和讨论，对这个赛事进行了解和熟悉，为下一步的介绍打下基础。

第四步：Develop 发展

本环节采用的是任务型教学法和情境教学法。首先，给学生展示了 WCG 现场的图片，要求学生模仿本课课文，运用关键句型以记者的身份(或代言人的身份)来介绍图片。这一环节的任务设置分为三个部分，即发展历史、地点和著名选手的介绍。学生可以任意选择一部分进行介绍。学生在其中锻炼了灵活运用所学内容的能力，并且细心的同学为介绍增加了很多新的内容，使整个 Development 更为灵活和丰满。

第五步：Evaluate 评价

在评价中引导学生注重细节。如课文中有一个句子是 The attention for the spectator is considerable. 但是学生在介绍 WCG 的时候，除了两侧的电子屏，似乎找不到其他相关的内容，于是教师在这里可以启发性地问一下学生：Where are the players? They are in two glass boxes. Why? 学生这时就会想到是方便观众观察选手。所以这种启发式的评价是非常有用的。

对用适当的连词如 so... that, in order to... 等把介绍连接得非常流利的学生给予高度的评价，这也是学生长期积累的结果，为今后的作文练习打下了良好的基础。

综上所述，本课在听说教学法的指导下，在每一个步骤采取了有针对性的教学法。学生通过快节奏地听，过渡到流利地说，从中还学习到了体育赛事的相关知识，可是说本节课是一堂快节奏、高容量的课。当然，本节课还有一些不足，如内容较多，比较适合程度很好的学生；节奏过快，留给学生消化和记忆的时间不够。这要求教师在今后教学环节的设计上更具针对性和灵活性。

Teaching Plan for Unit 10 Holidays
An Integrated English Course Book I

教师：董颜华

Teaching Aims:

1. To get the students to talk about what people do on Christmas.
2. To get the students to talk about the differences and similarities between Christmas and the Spring Festival.

Teaching Objects:

Students from Junior One.

Language Points:

Talk about activities on holidays.

Simple present tense.

Teaching Aids:

Tape-recorder, and multi-media teaching aid.

Teaching Methods:

1. Task-based Language Teaching Approach.
2. Audio-lingual Method.

Teaching Procedures

1. Greeting and duty report.

2. Guessing game.

(1) Ask the students what they usually do on holidays. Do people have interesting celebrations on holidays?

(2) Then the teacher show the students some pictures and let them guess what festival it is.

Activate

在课堂教学开始前的较短时间内灵活安排新颖的导入活动，促使全班学生集中注意力，迅速进入学习状态。

Halloween October 31st

Jack-o'lantern

apple-bobbing

fancy dress party

trick or treat

Easter A Sunday in March or April

Easter eggs

Easter bunny

roll eggs

lily

Mother's Day 2nd Sunday in May

<table>
<tr>
<td></td>
<td>
Thanksgiving Day 4th Thursday in November

turkey
Christmas

To the Westerners it is as important as the Spring Festival to the Chinese.
</td>
</tr>
<tr>
<td>
Build
运用综合教学方法指导教学设计，营造良好的学习氛围，使学生快乐、自然、轻松、有效地学习语言。
</td>
<td>
1. Talk about the symbols of Christmas.

Christmas carol
(1) When Christmas Comes to town
(2) Santa Claus Is Coming to Town
(3) We Wish You a Merry Christmas
(4) Silent Night
(5) Jingle Bells

</td>
</tr>
</table>

2. Listen and find out what people do to celebrate Christmas.

(1) Does the speaker like Christmas?

(2) What do people do on Christmas Day?

(3) What do people do on Christmas Eve?

Item 1. Listen to the passage and answer questions.

① **Does the speaker like Christmas?**

② **What does she do on Christmas Day?**

bake Christmas cookies	plan parties
send cards and hear from old friends	see children open their gifts

③ **What do they do on Christmas Eve?**

go from house to house	sing Christmas songs
drink hot chocolate	

Cultivate

按照启发式教学原则，设计饶有趣味的训练来充分调动学生学习的主动性。

1. Let the students talk about what else they know about Christmas.

What else do you know about Christmas?

Some people will attend church services on Christmas Eve.

Some people will watch the parades.

	2. Listen to the passage about the Spring Festival. Let the students listen to the passage and answer the questions. Help the students talk about what they know about the Spring Festival. Q1: When does the Spring Festival begin and end? Q2: What is every family busy doing before the Spring Festival? Why? Q3: Why do people let off firecrackers? Q4: What do people do on New Year's Eve? Q5: What do people do after the meal? Q6: What do the children receive?
Develop 设计真实的语言环境来综合概括构建及养成部分所传达的语言信息，巩固课堂教学、衔接新旧知识、贯通前后内容，帮助学生学习训练，复习巩固。	**Development Ⅰ** Find the similarities and differences between the Spring Festival and Christmas. **Development Ⅱ** We have already had a lot of holidays in China. If we can have one more holiday, who do you think it's for? When will it be? Why do we celebrate this holiday? How will you celebrate this holiday? …
Evaluate 评估教学活动的实际效果，分析学习成效，帮助学生排除学习障碍。	**Homework** (1) Recite Item 1. (2) Finish workbook Exercise 1, 2 and 3. **Teaching Reflection** Holiday is a very popular topic among the students. They are familiar with holidays in China and in the Western countries. The teacher used the guessing game to arouse the students' interest. Then the teacher designed lots of activities and also gave some listening materials for the students to practice. This enabled the students to talk about the differences and similarities between Christmas and the Spring Festival by using what they had learned. From the development we can see that the students know the cultural differences and can express their ideas freely. Most of the students are active in the class. How to stimulate all the students to take part in the activities should also be taken into consideration. The teacher should also pay attention to reading and writing practice.

课程设计及反思

教师：董颜华

本单元着重介绍国外节日习俗。本课为听说课，使用了任务型教学法。通过介绍圣诞节，让学生对圣诞节有更深入的了解。同时和中国的春节加以比较，使学生了解两种文化的共同点和差异。最后的活动为开放性的活动：我们还可以增加什么样的节日？这个替换和转换活动要求学生灵活运用所学知识，进一步锻炼学生说的能力，也使学生关注生活，关注社会。

☞ 教学步骤与反思：

在 Activate 环节中，首先进行了常规教学值日报告，锻炼学生的语言运用能力。

其次使用了游戏教学法。通过简单的猜节日的游戏，提高学生的兴趣。同时，引出本节课的话题——圣诞节，很好地调动了学生的积极性。

在 Build 环节中，首先提出问题：谈到圣诞节，我们会想到什么呢？让学生从他们熟悉的圣诞树、圣诞老人、圣诞歌等谈起，引导学生讨论圣诞节的活动。学生很轻松地参与到这个话题的讨论中，很好地激起了学生的兴趣。

其次采用了听说教学法。教师根据文章给出问题，学生听并回答问题。通过这个活动，既锻炼了学生听说的能力，也使学生对圣诞节的活动有了基本的认识。

在 Cultivate 环节中，教师设问：关于圣诞节，我们还知道什么呢？引导学生用自己的语言介绍关于圣诞节的其他活动及其他文化背景知识。部分学生能参与到这个话题的讨论中，这个话题有一定的难度，在具体操作上应有所改变，以便更多的学生能加入到讨论中。

最后采用了听说教学法。春节是中国的传统节日，学生对春节的庆祝方式很了解，但在表达方面可能存在一定困难。因此教师设置了关于春节的几段听力材料，让学生听并回答问题。教师把关键信息以文字的形式呈现出来，学生可以把听力材料的内容变为他们口头表达的素材，用“听”来输入，用“说”来输出，为本课的活动——圣诞节和春节的比较——做好铺垫。

Development 环节仍是听说教学活动的一个延续。要求学生能找到两种文化的异同点，能够运用本节课所操练的句型来表达自己熟悉的节日，即完成听说教学中的替换和转换。我们还可以增加什么样的节日？怎么庆祝？这是本节课的一个拓展活动，难度有所增加，进一步锻炼学生的语言创新能力及灵活运用能力。学生通过前面大量的听说活动，能够很好地运用所学句型来表达自己熟悉的东西，并能有所创新。通过最后的两个活动，我们可以说本节课基本达到了教师的预设目标，学生通过本节课的学习，能了解两种文化的差异，能对两种文化进行简单的比较，并锻炼了学生的语言运用能力。

在 Evaluate 环节中，教师布置作业并对本课进行反思。本节课基本达到了预设目标，但还有不太令人满意的地方：对所给听力材料的处理上还应斟酌，使它能更好地为自己的教学目标服务。课堂上还可以给学生更多的自由学习和交流的空间。

Teaching Plan of *Look, Listen and Learn* Book 3 Lesson 45 Television Day

教师：冯文力

Teaching Aims: 1. To get the students to know how to compare things in different aspects, such as colour, shape, size, height, quality, etc. 2. To get them to know how to make comparison.
Teaching Objects: Students in Junior Two.
Language Points: New words: exactly, object, compare, model Key structure: the same as, different in, different from
Teaching Aids: Audio-visual method, and blackboard.
Teaching Methods: 1. Communicative Approach. 2. Task-based Approach.

Teaching Procedures

Activate

在课堂教学开始前的较短时间内灵活安排新颖的导入活动，促使全班学生集中注意力，迅速进入学习状态。

Step 1 Duty report.
The history of APPLE Corporation.
Teacher's comment.

Step 2 The teacher's greeting and joking with one of the students.

"What if Lynette gives you an i-touch or an i-pad?" (She is very excited.)

"What if you lose it right after I give you?" (She turns sad.)

"One expresses his or her feelings by facial expressions. We have many kinds of that. Let's play a game to try to copy them and act them out."

<u>Game Copycats</u>

Rule: The students will be divided into several groups of five, we name the students A, B, C, D, E. The teacher will ask A to face the blackboard while the other students turn back to it. Then the teacher will show A a picture of facial expression and ask A to copy it (The other students can't see the picture until they finish the game). Then ask B to turn to A, A will act it out to B, and then B to C, C to D until we come to the last student E, and we will compare E's facial expression with the one in the picture to see whether it is the same, similar or different.

Questions like: Are they the same?
Are they different?

<table>
<tr>
<td></td>
<td>

</td>
</tr>
<tr>
<td>
Build

运用综合教学方法指导教学设计，营造良好的学习氛围，使学生快乐、自然、轻松、有效地学习语言。
</td>
<td>
Step 1　See the PPT.
Let's compare something.
For example：Show them two books.
The books are <u>different from</u> each other <u>in color</u>.
The books are <u>not the same color</u> (as each other).
Also size, build, weight, height, price, quality, appearance, etc.
The teacher provide different pictures for the students to practice.

</td>
</tr>
</table>

They are different in price.

They are different in apperance.

They are not the same quality.

Step 2 See the PPT.

We can see many differences in our daily life and sometimes those differences can bring us surprise and beauty. Or sometimes we even create differences.

Look at this mouse, is it cute? How about this one? (Mickey Mouse) Can you tell me the differences between them and the things they have in common?

The mickey mouse is not a real character, it is a kind of creation. We call it art, the one who makes it is an artist. Let's see more works of art like this.

Sometimes artists copy the things exactly, but sometimes they don't, they make changes.

We have another artist in our programme, too. Let's listen and see whether he copies exactly or not?

	Text Learning

a. Listen and take down notes.

- **What did the artist use as a model?**
  And what did they often use as models?
- **What did the artist do?**
  Did he copy them exactly?

How many more differences are there in the picture?

*C*ultivate

按照启发式教学原则，设计饶有趣味的训练来充分调动学生学习的主动性。

b. Listen again and repeat, then fill in the blanks. (Books closed)

In our programme today, we want you to __________ two pictures. On the left, you can see some __________. Our artist used these __________. On the right, you can see a picture. Our artist drew it for you. Did the artist copy the objects __________? Of course, not. The pictures are __________ each other. For instance, the bowl in the picture on the left isn't __________ the one on the right. Artists often use __________ as models, but they don't always __________ them exactly. Compare the two pictures __________. There are five more __________. Can you find them all?

TV Commentary

In our programme today, we want you to __compare__ two pictures. On the left, you can see some __objects__

Our artist used these __as a model__.
On the right, you can see a picture. Our artist drew it for you.
Did the artist copy the objects __exactly__? Of course, not.
The pictures are __different from__ each other.
For instance, the bowl in the picture on the left isn't __the same shape as__ the one on the right.
Artists often use __real people and real things__ as models, but they don't always __copy__ them exactly.
Compare the two pictures __carefully__.
There are five more __differences__.
Can you find them all?

c. Listen again and read. (Books open)

Develop

设计真实的语言环境来综合概括构建及养成部分所传达的语言信息，巩固课堂教学、衔接新旧知识、贯通前后内容，帮助学生学习训练，复习巩固。

We have many kinds of copies, can you tell me what else you can copy?

Different Kinds of Copies

- False currency(fake money), fake tickets
- Copycat, such as copying the homework and papers,cheating in the exams
- Pirate copy, such as books, DVDs, software
- Cheap Copy
- Models

Ask the students to talk about them in details.
Discuss in groups and make a presentation.
**How do they compare to the real ones?
Tips: Try to use "different from (in), the same as, as much as possible." You can gain extra points.

Evaluate

评估教学活动的实际效果，分析学习成效，帮助学生排除学习障碍。

相当于教学反思并布置作业。

1. Give marks to the correct sentences during each group's presentation.
   If they use "be different in, different from, the same as". They can get one more point for each sentence.
   And we can see some excellent students can talk frequently for more than 5 sentences, even those who are not good at English can say a few sentences and gain some points.
2. Summary: We have learnt how to compare two things in different aspects today. What's more, we can use it in our daily conversation.
3. Homework: a. Recite Lesson 45.
   b. Finish the workbook of Lesson 45.

课程设计及反思

教师：冯文力

我这节课选取了上海外语教育出版社和朗文出版的《看听学》第三册的第 45 课 Television Day，这是一节听说阅读课。

本课的教学目的是让学生掌握 the same as... 和 different in/from... 这两个句型，并将其结合以前所学的有关比较的知识，让他们进一步学会如何去比较不同的事物，我采取了任务和交际教学法以及 ABCDE 五步教学模式设计课堂。

第一步，激活环节，首先是当日值日学生的 duty report。为了活跃气氛，让孩子们放松起来，我使用了趣味游戏教学法，在开始的时候我设置了游戏 copycats，游戏的内容及方法也根据班级学生的特点而进行了适当调整。由游戏引出 the same 和 different 这两个关键词。

第二步，构建环节，展示不同的图片，以填空的形式让他们比较颜色、大小、高矮、重量，在复习已学过的比较级内容的同时，引出目标句型 different from...in，the same as，通过 3 ~4 幅图让他们熟悉句型，然后逐步加大练习难度，这部分的练习主要针对程度一般或者较差的同学。运用了直接教学法。

接着深入扩展，提高句型操练的难度。通过比较学生熟悉的卡通形象，来进一步让他们进行口语练习，说出卡通形象和他们原形的区别。

借着上一个部分卡通形象和原形的比较，导出 works of art 以及 artist 这个文本里的关键词，引出艺术家在创作的时候有时也会刻意有一些改变，为导入课文做好铺垫。

第三步，养成环节，在文本处理部分，首先让学生在关书的情况下听一遍，对课文内容有大致的了解，回答一系列较简单的问题。关书听第二遍课文，完成课文原文填空。第三遍，开书听课文跟读，进一步让学生熟悉课文。学生练习了听和读，收到了不错的效果。

第四步，发展环节，学生了解课文内容之后，侧重点在 copy 这个词上，引出拓展部分，让学生对不同类型的 copy 展开讨论，教师给予引导，让他们从日常生活实际中发现更多的不同，锻炼了学生的思维能力，同时也更好地锻炼了他们的口语能力。在这个过程中，我也采取了量化的方式，凡是采用了所学句型的学生得到双倍的分数，也进一步调动了他们的积极性。

第五步，评价环节，由于拓展的内容和生活离得很近，学生也乐于开口说。最后的量化也使得他们更加有竞争意识。积极性得到很好的调动。作业布置也旨在以指导性作文方式复习当天的学习内容。

在课后，我进行了教学反思：

1. 教学过程中要不断将正在学习的知识与技能融入要完成的任务中，也就是在新学的知识、技能与运用任务之间建立直接的关联，使学生既掌握知识与技能，更形成运用这些知识与技能的能力。

2. 在处理文本方面，难度区分很明显，目标很明确。任务型教学完成得很成功。

3. 在拓展部分，学生的口语得到了很好的锻炼，我选择的方向是他们感兴趣的，因此积极性调动得很好，另外由于和生活离得很近，学生也乐于开口说。最后的量化也使得他们更加有竞争意识。

4. 另外，教师的语言很重要，比如，游戏的指示语言要明确，简单清晰，便于学生理解，以鼓励和赞赏为主。我在这方面处理也比较得当。

任务型教学法

任务型教学法

向　阳

一、任务型教学法的定义

任务型教学(Task-based Language Teaching)是指教师通过引导语言学习者在课堂上完成任务来进行的教学。这是20世纪80年代兴起的一种强调“在做中学”(learning by doing)的语言教学方法，是交际教学法的发展，在世界语言教育界引起了人们的广泛注意。近年来，这种“用语言做事”(doing things with the language)的教学理论逐渐被引入到我国的基础英语课堂教学中来，是我国外语课程教学改革的一个走向。任务型教学理论认为：掌握语言大多是在活动中使用语言的结果，而不是单纯训练语言技能和学习语言知识的结果。在教学活动中，教师应当围绕特定的交际话题和语言项目，设计出具体的、可操作的任务，使得学生通过表达、沟通、交涉、解释、询问等各种语言活动形式来完成任务，以达到学习和掌握语言的目的。

二、任务型教学法的历史

美国教育家杜威根据教育理论，提出了“以学生为中心，在做中学”的教育模式。他主张教育的中心应从教师和教科书转到学生，教学过程应是引导学生在各种活动中学习的过程。语言学家Herbort H. Clark(1996)说：“Language is for doing things.”学习语言既不是背诵单个的单词，也不是熟记脱离语境的句子，更不是记忆枯燥乏味的语法规则，而应当教会学生用恰当的语言把要做的事情做好，词汇和语法都是为“做事情”和“完成任务”服务的，课堂上教师的任务就是在语言运用的活动中把词汇、语法和功能项目有机地结合起来。20世纪70年代，N. S. Prabhu在印度进行了一项交际法的实验(Bargalore Project)，他提出了许多任务类型，并把学习的内容设计成各种交际任务，让学生通过完成任务进行学习。

三、任务型教学法在外校的应用

任务型课堂教学就是把课堂活动任务化，以任务为核心计划教学步骤，所以任务设计的质量是一堂课成败的关键。设计的任务应具有挑战性，能让学生体验成功。所以作为站在教学一线的外语教师，我们必须认真做好学生需要分析，切实了解学生想做什么，会做什么，该做什么，设计能学以致用、与生活有关、促进学生全面发展的任务。武汉实验外国语学校的英语教师在课堂教学中大量引入任务型教学法的理念来设计教学活动。下面以三名实验外国语学校英语教师的授课实例说明任务型教学法如何在外校的课堂上得以应用。

范例一：梁静老师在 *IEC* Book 3 Unit 4 Dialogue 2 的教学设计中，在激活、构建、发展环节中都使用到了任务型教学法。例如在发展环节中，她提出一个任务，要求学生们以分组讨论的形式在他们观看过的部分原版影片中选出各奖项得主，并模拟仪式现场致颁奖词，对该获奖影片做出点评，训练说的技能。因此学生不得不在任务的驱动下内化刚学到的句型并进行反复操练。最后由场景模拟阶段进入评价环节——让学生进行相互交流，将自己或小组完成任务的过程和所得出的结论向其他学生作报告。一个由学生自己组织的奥斯卡模拟颁奖典礼的任务得以完成。

范例二：任瑶瑶老师选用了 *IEC* Unit 10 Holidays Item 1 作为自己教学的展示，她对于任务型教学方法的应用主要体现在发展环节中。首先她要求学生把自己假想成一位名人，做圣诞节计划，让学生在这个任务的驱动下去用语言做事。然后学生进入准备阶段，相互讨论该名人会如何度过圣诞节以弥补信息差，经由这个环节进入到最后的报告阶段，以小组的形式来表演自己的圣诞节安排，以此完成一个真实场景下的以明确任务为向导的语言交际活动。在这个活动中教师要求学生通过完成任务的学习活动掌握真实、实用和有意义的语言。

范例三：向阳老师在 *IEC* Unit 7 Item 1 的教学中呈现了典型的任务性教学手段。首先她模拟和学生进行电话沟通的场景，并要求学生记一个电话留言，因为学生的语言输入里暂时没有电话留言记载的有效模板或规则，学生在黑板上展示的留言丰富多样，但没有任何一个是正确有效的。此时学生就发现在真实的情境中自己用英语做事方面的不足，因此具备了较强的任务达成驱动力。因此向阳老师进入下一阶段，即任务准备阶段：知识与技能教学。任务准备过程实际上就是我们的课堂构建和养成过程。向阳老师通过 PPT 视频的演示首先向学生呈现了一个有效的记录留言的模板，然后通过在黑板上板书进行教学并要求学生进行技能训练。最后进入到任务完成阶段，向阳老师选择在课堂上要求学生完成记录电话留言的任务，并给出生病请假、生日聚会等符合学生年龄阶段常用的真实情境，引导学生完成任务并进行展示。

四、任务型教学法在应用上的不足

任务型教学法要求学生运用所学语言完成具体任务，并强调学生的主动参与，它强调交际的过程和语言的功能，注重发展学生的学习策略，因而有利于提高学生的创新精神和语言运用能力。当然，任务型教学在初中阶段的教学应用中存在一些不完备的地方：

1．任务的指令语言必须要明晰清楚。必要情况下教师要花一定量的时间做解释；

2．任务的等级评定并没有量化。到底什么是任务的达成？是功能性的还是语言结构层次上的？如何去评定学生任务的达成水平？

Teaching Plan of *IEC* Book 3 Unit 4 Dialogue 2

教师：梁静

Teaching Aims:

1. The students will learn how to give comments on films.
2. The students will understand "One strand of silk doesn't make a thread; one tree doesn't make a forest."

Teaching Objects:

Junior Two Students in WEFLS.

Language Points:

1. Different kinds of films.
2. Giving comments by using adjectives.

Teaching Aids:

A multi-media computer, a recorder, and a tape.

Teaching Methods:

1. Communicative Approach.
2. Task-based Approach.

Teaching Procedures

	1. Greeting and duty report. 2. Play the game "A-Z" about movies. The teacher gives the first letter and ask the Ss to list words about movies (e. g. a = actor/ actress/ animation/ action movie, etc.).

<table>
<tr>
<td>Activate

在课堂教学开始前的较短时间内灵活安排新颖的导入活动，促使全班学生集中注意力，迅速进入学习状态。</td>
<td>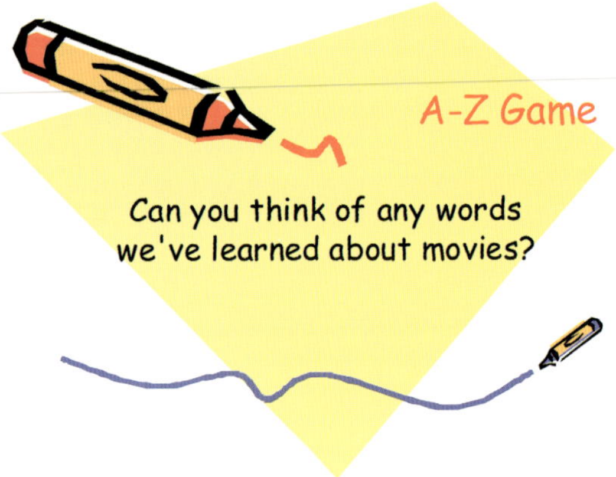
</td>
</tr>
<tr>
<td>Build

运用综合教学方法指导教学设计，营造良好的学习氛围，使学生快乐、自然、轻松、有效地学习语言。</td>
<td>3. Show posters of the movies the Ss have seen. Ask the Ss to say what kinds of movies they are and what they think of the movies. Encourage them to use adjectives for giving opinions. Learn some new words and expressions such as special effect, moving, be impressed with, etc.

</td>
</tr>
</table>

musical
HIGH SCHOOL MUSICAL 3
SENIOR YEAR
ONLY IN CINEMAS
FROM WEDS 22 OCT

science-fiction movie
(sci-fi movie)
STAR WARS
EPISODE III
MAY 19

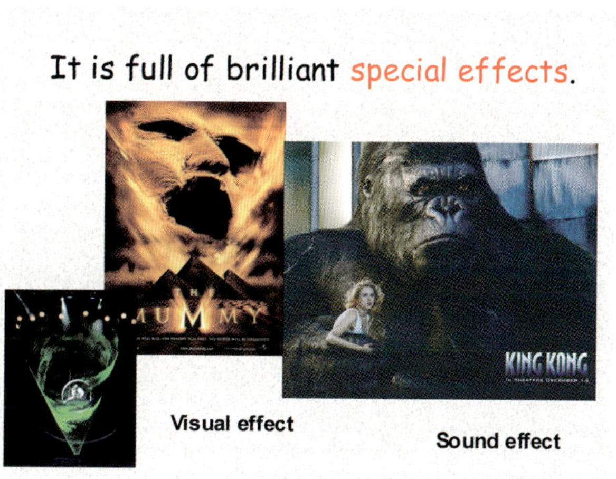
It is full of brilliant special effects.
THE MUMMY
KING KONG
Visual effect
Sound effect

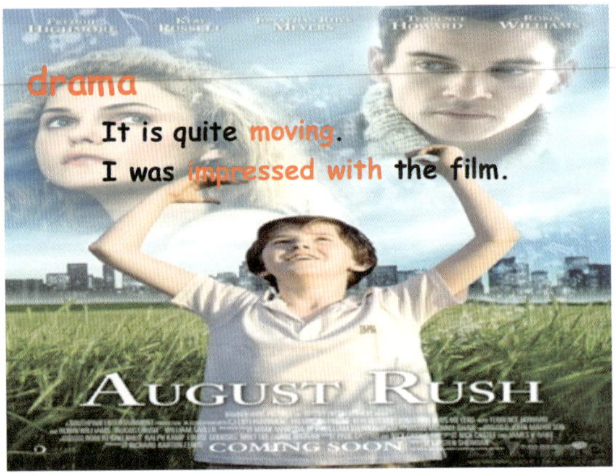

4. The most important event for movies every year is OSCARS. Which movie was the biggest winner for the 81st OSCARS?

Slumdog Millionaire got 8 prizes. However, it didn't get the "Best Actor".

A movie with 5 prizes including the “Best Actor”.

Which film was it?

Cultivate

按照启发式教学原则，设计饶有趣味的训练来充分调动学生学习的主动性。

5. Text studying.

(1) Listen to the dialogue and answer the questions. Books shut.

Listening questions

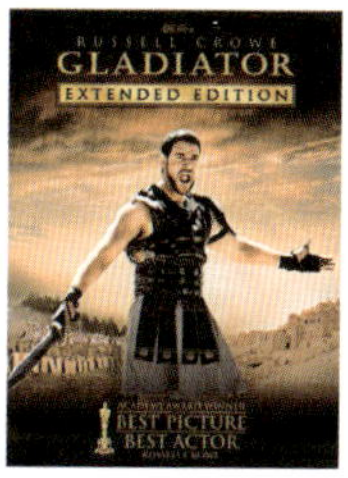

1. What was the name of the film?
   It was *Gladiator*.
2. Who was the actor?
   Russel Crowe was the gladiator.
3. Did the woman like the film? How do you know that?
   Yes, she did.
   "I really like it. It was full of brilliant special effects."
   "His acting was very good. I was impressed. It is quite moving."

n. (in ancient Rome and Etruria) a man trained to fight in arenas to provide entertainment

(2) Listen to and repeat after the tape, first in groups, then individually. Books open.

(3) Show the Ss some other comments on ***Gladiator***. Do the audience like the movie?

<table>
<tr>
<td></td>
<td>

Comments on *Gladiator*

- Great Story! Great Writing! Great Acting! Great Directing! Great Score! This movie has it all.
- It will be well worth your time and money.
- Why Russell Crowe? He's not the one for the film.
- One of the greatest movie I've ever seen. You can't miss it.
- Special effects and powerful acting makes the film a poem.
- When death stares at you and smiles, all you can do is smile back.
- It's a big NO NO. I just slept through.

6. Giving comments.
   How to give comments on movies by using adjectives or simple sentences? Ask the Ss to find examples in the dialogue, and then add some more.

- I really like it. It was full of brilliant special effects.
- The acting was very good. I was impressed.
- It is quite moving.
- Great Story! Great Writing! Great Acting! Great Directing! Great Score! This movie has it all.
- It will be well worth your time and money.
- One of the greatest movie I've ever seen. You can't miss it.
- Special effects and powerful acting makes the film a poem.

</td>
</tr>
<tr>
<td>

*D*evelop

设计真实的语言环境来综合概括构建及养成部分所传达的语言信息，巩固课堂教学、衔接新旧知识、贯通前后内容，帮助学生学习训练，复习巩固。

</td>
<td>

7. Group work: The OSCARS of Junior 2.
   Ask the Ss to work in groups. Each group gives a prize and their comments. Write down the comments and give a presentation.

</td>
</tr>
</table>

8. Discussion: Which factor is the most important for a well-made movie? Moral: One strand of silk doesn't make a thread; one tree doesn't make a forest.

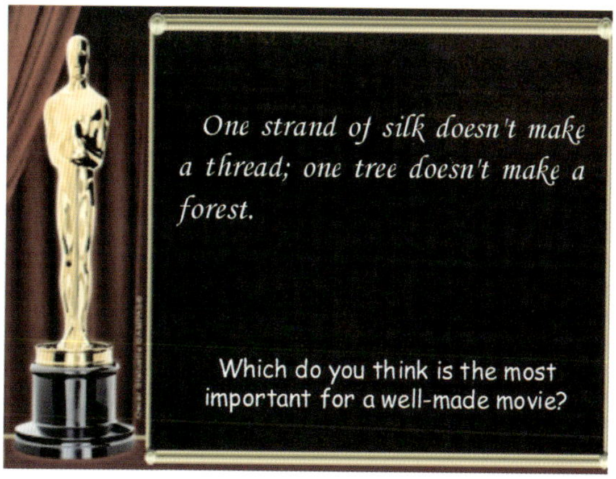

*E*valuate 评估教学活动的实际效果，分析学习成效，帮助学生排除学习障碍。	So far the Ss have had the idea of how to give comments by using the target language as well as some basic language knowledge needed while doing so. In the activities above, they were able to fulfill the tasks and gave a final presentation really well. The aims of this class have be successfully achieved. 9. Homework. 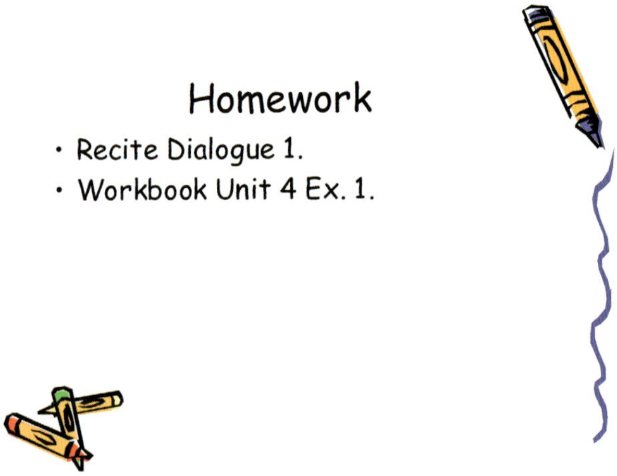

课程设计及反思

教师：梁静

本课选取了“全国外国语学校系列教材”《英语综合教程》第三册第四单元的对话 2，是一节以听说为主，兼顾读写的课。

本节课的教学目的是使学生初步掌握如何对一部电影做出简单的评价。课件图文信息量大，在词汇量、理解能力及对句型的灵活运用方面对学生的要求较高。

在教学中，我主要使用了游戏教学法、任务型教学法和情景教学法。

在 Activate 环节中，我使用了游戏教学法，给出从 A 至 Z 的首字母，让学生们快速反应，任意说出由该字母开头的与电影相关的单词。这项单词联想游戏为学生做好了对本课所需词汇的预热。由于该游戏可有多个答案，学生们的积极性很容易被调动，制造出轻松的课堂气氛有利于后期学习性任务和真实生活任务的开展。

Build 环节是任务型教学法的“任务呈现”和“任务准备——知识学习”阶段，分为两部分操作。在第一部分，先回顾学生在影视欣赏课所看过的原版电影，用问答的方式对电影类型的相关词汇和学生们已经学过的表达个人观点的句型进行复习，同时引入课文中出现的生词新句。从词到句，由浅入深，这么做符合认知和学习的规律，高速紧凑的刺激方式让学生的注意力更加集中。在第二部分，我由第 81 届奥斯卡颁奖典礼的最大赢家《贫民窟的百万富翁》错过“最佳男主角奖”过渡到此奖项曾经的得主《角斗士》，从实例引入课文，让语言贴近生活，这么做容易引起学生的兴趣，使到课文的过渡更加自然。

Cultivate 环节属于任务型教学法的“任务准备——技能训练”阶段。我让学生们在课本未打开的前提下听课文对话，理解大意并回答问题，训练听的技能。在跟读课文的过程中，我通过集体跟读和个人跟读，强化学生对生词和新学句式的重复操练，加深学生的印象。然后，我请学生们找出文中关于电影评价的词句，总结归纳如何使用语言的评价功能并给出其他相关评价句式，提示学生注意理解文本，注重评价的客观性，训练读的技能。同时为后期的语言运用环节做了句型方面的进一步准备。

在 Develop 环节中，我结合情景教学法设计了一个小型的年级奥斯卡颁奖典礼，呈现了任务型教学法的“任务完成”阶段。我要求学生们以分组讨论的形式在所观看过的部分原版影片中选出各奖项得主，并模拟仪式现场致颁奖词，对该获奖影片做出点评，训练学生说的技能。为了使参与面更广，我给了学生们一定的准备时间并要求他们在规定时间内写好颁奖词，训练了他们写的技能。

英语课程的学习除了掌握语言知识与技能、提高语言实际运用能力之外，还应注意培养学生们积极的情感态度。在 Develop 环节的最后阶段，我让学生回答在一部好的电影中哪个因素是最重要的。学生们经过讨论得出：独木不成林，团队合作是成功的关键。这种愉快的情感体验有利于学生们保持积极的学习态度、形成健康的人生观。

以“颁奖典礼”形式呈现的检测活动格调高雅且不失活泼，课件中恰当的视觉音效设计营造出颁奖现场的热烈气氛，让学生们有很强的表达欲望。学生们在致辞中自然运用所学词句对该影片做出评价，自觉运用语言于生活，取得了较好的效果，Evaluate 的结论：达到了预定教学目标。

Teaching Plan of *An Integrated English Course* Book 1 Unit 10 Holidays Item 1

教师：任瑶瑶

Teaching Aims:

1. Knowledge aims: to get the students to master some new words about Christmas and future plans.
2. Ability aims: to enable the students to make a Christmas plan.
3. Emotional aims: to get the students to know that Christmas is a time to share a good fortune with others.

Teaching Objects:

Junior One.

Language Points:

decorate, by the fireplace, wrap up gifts, sleigh, Christmas carols, carolers, go caroling, go to church, hear from sb., afterwards, be going to

Teaching Aids:

The multi-media equipments, a tape-recorder, handouts, and some exercise-books as gifts.

Teaching Methods:

1. Task-based Approach.
2. Communicative Approach.

Teaching Procedures

Activate 在课堂教学开始前的较短时间内灵活安排新颖的导入活动，促使全班学生集中注意力，迅速进入学习状态。	**Step 1　Duty report.** Some background knowledge about Christmas. **Step 2　A game "Grace says".** All the students stand up. If I say "Grace says touch your noses", they should do that. If I only say "touch your nose", they shouldn't move. If they make a mistake, they should sit down. The winners will get exercise-books as Christmas gifts.
Build 运用综合教学方法指导教学设计，营造良好的学习氛围，使学生快乐、自然、轻松、有效地学习语言。	**Step 3** 1. Use some pictures with the teacher's explanation to teach the students all the new words and expressions in Item 1 and the video. And also talk about some activities at Christmas.  

Father Christmas
Santa Claus
Santa
St. Nicolas
reindeer
sleigh

carollers
go from house to house
in the neighbourhood
sing Christmas carols
at each house
go carolling

go to church

2. Make a conclusion. What do western people do at Christmas? (according to what we talked about just now)

What else do they do? (according to your experience)

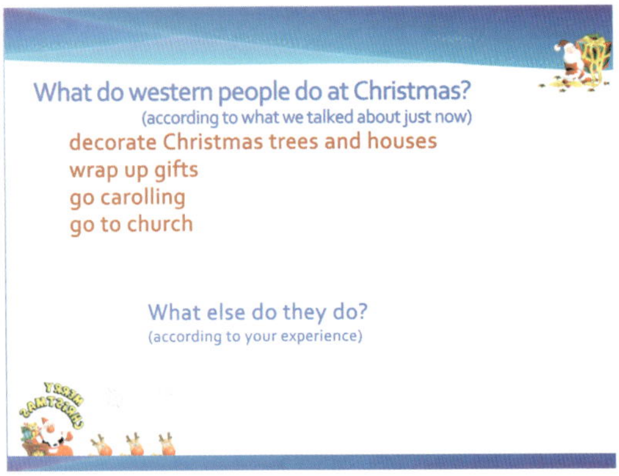

Step 4 Listen to Item 1 and answer the question.

1. Listen and list the speaker's activities at Christmas.

2. Listen and repeat. (chorus and individual)

Step 5　A video.

Watch the video and just get the main idea about the four American students' Christmas plans.

Task 1. Match the people with their Christmas plans.

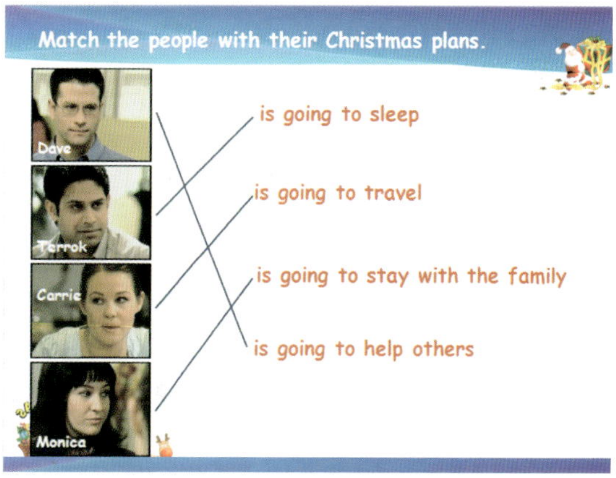

*C*ultivate

按照启发式教学原则，设计饶有趣味的训练来充分调动学生学习的主动性。

<table>
<tr>
<td></td>
<td>

Task 2. Fill in the blanks. (play the video in sections)

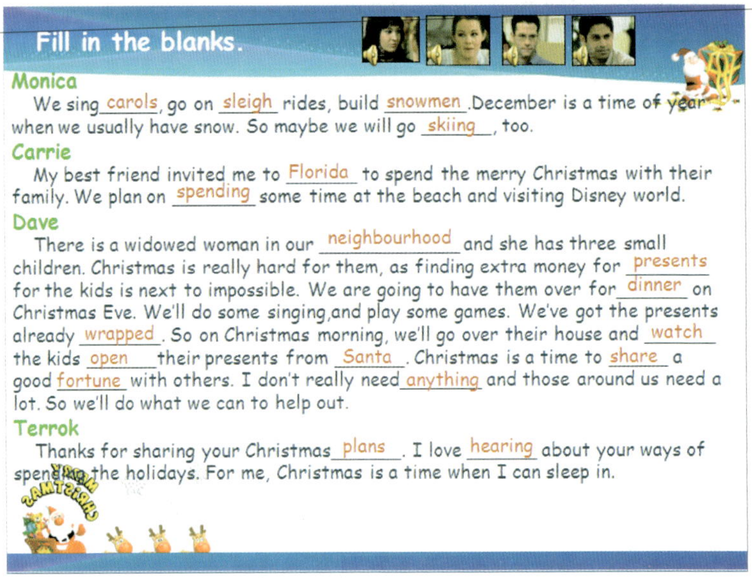

</td>
</tr>
<tr>
<td>

Develop

设计真实的语言环境来综合概括构建及养成部分所传达的语言信息，巩固课堂教学、衔接新旧知识、贯通前后内容，帮助学生学习训练，复习巩固。

</td>
<td>

Step 6 Role-play.

Different people will spend Christmas in very different ways. Present the students the pictures of Santa, Justin Bieber, their maths teacher, their American teacher and Bill Gates. Divide the students into five groups and the group leaders draw lots to decide for whom they are going to make a Christmas plan. Each group is responsible for one person. Give the students four minutes to prepare and then have the presentation. They should start like this: I am Justin Bieber. This Christmas, I am going to …

</td>
</tr>
</table>

Evaluate 评估教学活动的实际效果，分析学习成效，帮助学生排除学习障碍。	**Step 7　Homework** Read and recite Item 1. Workbook Unit 10 Exercise 1-4. **Teaching Reflection** The teacher made good use of 45 minutes to get the students to practise their listening, speaking, reading and writing. And all the teaching aims are achieved.

课程设计及反思

教师：任瑶瑶

我这节课选取了《综合英语》教材第一册第10单元的Item 1部分，是一节听说课。这节课的教学目的在文化方面是让学生熟知西方圣诞节的传统过法以及重要的圣诞元素，在交际方面是让学生能够熟练表达圣诞节计划，在语法方面是让学生能熟练运用一般将来时。圣诞节计划的主线十分清晰，所有活动都围绕这一主线展开。

我这节课使用了交际教学法和任务型教学法。交际教学法贯穿课堂，整节课都是在师生之间和学生之间直接地交流和对话中完成的。在Build（构建）部分重点用到了交际教学法，通过和学生之间轻松地谈论圣诞节的有关话题，一步步地呈现圣诞的重要元素以及目标词汇（词汇来自课文和补充的视听材料）。这个环节看似不经意地谈论，但是却让学生能够了解和掌握一部分目标知识，为接下来的任务打下基础。

任务型教学在这节课重点体现在Cultivate（养成）和Develop（发展）两个环节中。养成环节是通过看一段视频（视频是四个美国大学生谈论圣诞计划），完成两个难易不同的任务，第一个任务很简单，全班同学都能在看完视频后完成。第二个任务是将视频材料转换成音频材料，并按人物截成小段，配套设计了一套听力填空题。这个任务有难度，程度好的学生能够完成所有的题，反之则需反复听，才能完成。因此这段视频材料需要再做取舍，优化使用。学生通过这个任务了解了不同的人有不同的过圣诞节的方式，并且补充了一些语言元素。发展环节是做圣诞节计划。我给出五个学生所熟悉的人物，将学生分成五组，每组抽签决定他们将代表的人物，假设学生就是这个人物来做圣诞计划。这个任务需要学生用到当堂所学的知识以及创意去完成。这极大地引起了学生的兴趣，因为作为学生，他们的圣诞节过得比较雷同且受限制，没有什么特别的地方可以去谈论，而让他们去扮演不同的人物，情况就大不相同了，他们会有很多想法。学生的思维很发散，没有完全运用当堂所学的目标词汇，却很好地用到了将来时去表达自己的圣诞计划。

这节课各个环节衔接过渡比较流畅自然，能够层层递进。不同程度的学生在原有基础上都有进步。知识、能力、思想情操目标达成。同时，有效利用了课内的45分钟，学生学得轻松愉快，积极性高，当堂问题当堂解决，信息输入量充足，但学生负担比较合理，并没有过度，他们得到了锻炼。

Teaching Plan of *An Integrated English Course* Book 1 Unit 7 Item 1 A Telephone Call

教师：向阳

Teaching Aims:

Linguistic aims:

1. Enable the students to take messages on the phone in English if necessary.
2. Enable the students to make telephone calls that need them to take notes.

Moral aims:

Enable the students to have good cooperation with one another and make calls to people around them, especially the ones they need to show their love, such as parents or grandparents.

Teaching Objects:

The students of Grade 7.

Language Points:

leave a message, hold on, I've got it, call back

Teaching Aids:

The multi-media equipments, and a hat with the brand of "McDonald's" on it.

Teaching Methods:

1. Task-based Approach.
2. Situational Approach.

Teaching Procedures

<table>
<tr>
<td>

Activate

在课堂教学开始前的较短时间内灵活安排新颖的导入活动，促使全班学生集中注意力，迅速进入学习状态。

</td>
<td>

Warming up

Game: Can you memorize those numbers?

1. Ask 4 students to come to the front and name them individually from 5 to 8.
Tell the number 8756 7855 and ask them to jump and repeat the number.
2. Ask the number 8 student to stay and get other volunteers to be numbered 1 to 4 this time.
Tell the number 8142 3131 and ask them to jump and repeat the number.
3. Give the number 1384 2183 2222 and ask them to jump and repeat the number.

</td>
</tr>
<tr>
<td></td>
<td>

1. Watch the video and answer the questions.
Question 1: What are the messages for Cathy?
Question 2: How to take a message?
We should write it down.

</td>
</tr>
</table>

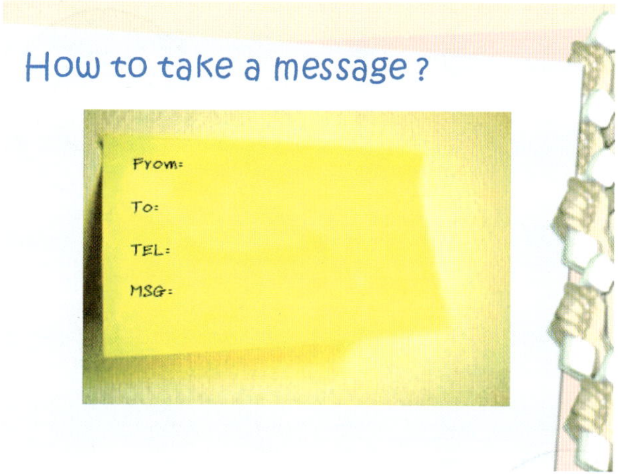

*B*uild

运用综合教学方法指导教学设计，营造良好的学习氛围，使学生快乐、自然、轻松、有效地学习语言。

T：(name a student) So you think we should write the message down to take it, then come to the blackboard and take a message for me!

S：OK.

Then teacher calls the student and leave a message.

Of course the student cannot take the message well without the guidance.

Have another student who believe he can do better to come up and have a try.

Then write the right way to take a message on the blackboard：

From：__________ To：__________

Tel：__________________________

MSG：__________________________

Give students another message to have a try and invite a student to do it on the blackboard to check if the students have master the way or not.

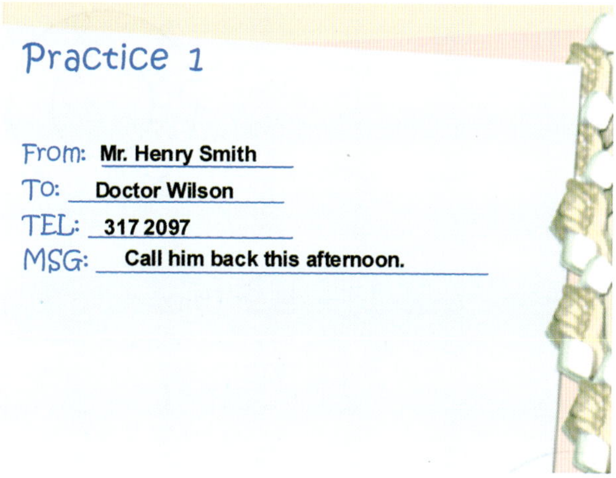

<table>
<tr>
<td></td>
<td>
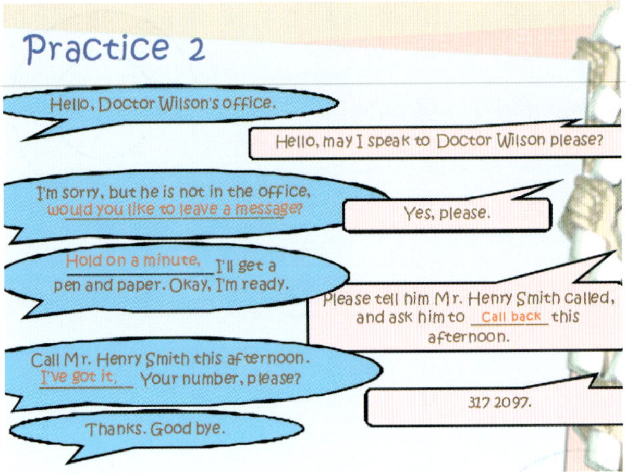

1. Listen to the tape and take the message.
2. Listen to the tape and fill in the missing message.
3. Read after the tape.
4. Read after the tape and explain expressions on the blackboard:
(1) hold on a minute=wait a minute; just a minute
(2) I've got it. = I've done it.
Ask the students to repeat after the teacher for three times.
</td>
</tr>
<tr>
<td>
Cultivate
按照启发式教学原则，设计饶有趣味的训练来充分调动学生学习的主动性。
</td>
<td>

Show the students a picture: The students in Class 4 are doing morning exercises.
Also give them a message, and ask them to make a call by the message.
Ask them to come up and show.
</td>
</tr>
</table>

From: ____________ To: ____________

Tel : ________________________

MSG: Do exercises.

Meet ____________ in the playground at ____________.

Don't be late!

Mum

Expressions you may need:

Leave a message.

Hold on a minute.

I've got it.

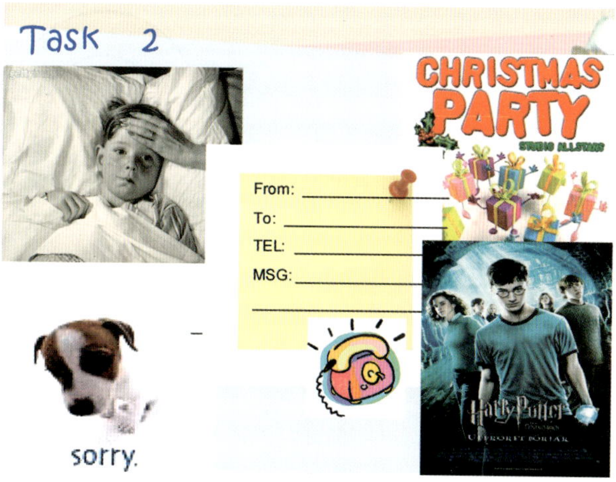

Leave a message that has nothing on it and ask the students to make a new call on their own.

Give them some situations like illness, parties, etc., by showing pictures.

From: ____________ To: ____________

Tel: ______________________________

MSG: ______________________________

Develop 设计真实的语言环境来综合概括构建及养成部分所传达的语言信息，巩固课堂教学、衔接新旧知识、贯通前后内容，帮助学生学习训练，复习巩固。	Show the students the foods in McDonald's and ask them what they should do if they are hungry and don't want to get out to buy the food? Get the answer that we can call the Mc Delivery because they just need to call and leave a message then the food will be delivered. There are 4 groups in class, in each group, there are people who called and leave a message about the food they want to have, and also the receptionist who picks up the phone and take the message. Also there must be Mc Delivery man who read the message and send the food. Give the students some time to practice and show. Judge and choose the best. 
Evaluate 评估教学活动的实际效果，分析学习成效，帮助学生排除学习障碍。	Teacher gives some comments on the students' performance and the homework.

课程设计及反思

教师：向阳

这节课选取了“全国外国语学校系列教材”《英语综合教程》第一册第七单元的 Item One 部分，是一节听说课。

教学目的：

语言知识、技能、策略方面：

1．用所学的电话用语通过电话这一媒介与人进行交流，在必要的情况下准确而迅速地记下对方的电话留言。

2．如何进行留言。

本课使用了全身反应法、听说法、视听法、交际法和任务型教学法。

具体步骤：

1．Activate 激活——全身反应教学法

教师匠心独具、巧妙创设的热身活动能在最短时间内唤起学生的好奇心和求知欲望，转移学生的兴奋点和注意力，帮助明确本课的学习目标。为了达到以上效果，教师充分考虑了初中一年级年龄段孩子的特点，设计了一个需要学生到讲台前来参与，跟其他同学配合有节奏地蹦蹦跳跳复述电话号码的游戏。这项活动的设计概念源于盛行于 20 世纪 70 年代的全身反应法。

在本课的教学中，教师发号指令(一个 8 位数的电话号码)，孩子们通过依次边跳跃边喊出自己所代表的那个数字的方式来复述教师给出的电话号码。上台参加活动的孩子们在没有压力的情况下既注意力高度集中地参与了活动，也激发了其他孩子的兴趣，同时也明朗了打电话这个教学重点，达到了预期的目的。

2．Build 构建

教师对于“什么是电话留言？怎样去进行电话留言？”的呈现，使用的是视听法。

视听结合的方法比单纯依靠听觉或视觉来理解、记忆和储存语言材料要好得多。视觉形象为学生提供形象思维的条件，促使学生自然和牢固地掌握外语。听觉形象有助于学生形成正确的语音、语调、节奏及遣词、造句的能力和习惯，同时有利于使课堂变得生动活泼，使学生学的语言自然，表达准确。在本课的教学中，教师对于留言概念的呈现正是利用了一段英国人日常生活中所进行的电话留言的视频，高效地呈现了一个好的电话留言的标准。

3. Cultivate 养成

电话沟通用语的习得——听说法

为了给学生足够的电话用语的语料输入，教师反复播放纯正流利的英语对话磁带并要求学生配合跟读模仿。为下一阶段的输出做准备。

4. 打电话的操练——交际法

交际法认为，语言是人们交际的工具。本堂课是一节听说课，因此教师在学生的操练中按照从易到难的顺序设计了两个活动——给同学打电话以及在不同的情境中给老师、朋友、家长打电话。通过活动的设置，教师从学生的生活和学习实际出发，使教学过程交际化，培养了学生综合运用语言的能力。

5. Develop 发展

拓展活动的设计——任务教学法

通过完成多种多样的任务，有助于激发学生的学习兴趣。在完成任务的过程中，将语言知识和语言技能结合起来，因此有利于促进学生积极参与语言交流活动，激发想象力和创造性思维，发挥学生的主体性作用。在本课的拓展活动中，学生被要求扮演麦当劳接话员、送餐员以及顾客的角色，完成包括打电话订餐、留言、确认点餐内容等一系列活动。学生在完成任务的同时也实现了语言知识的内化。

6. Evaluate 评价

教师通过开放式的提问对学生掌握本课内容的程度有一个评估，并通过布置作业深化了这一过程。

☞ 教学反思：

1. 全身反应法的应用

如果教师能把“发号施令”的“特权”多多下放到学生手中，相信学生通过这样的语言游戏，一定可以达到参与度更高、寓教于乐的目的。

2. 任务型教学法的应用

通过任务型教学法的使用，教师突出了语言教学的真实性和实践性。例如让学生自己表现如何在生活中留便条，如何准确无误地打电话订餐，鼓励和引导学生大胆参与语言学习和实践，借此培养学生听、说、读、写多方面的综合技能。任务型教学法综合了许多教学法的优点，因此教师可考虑更频繁地加以利用。

直接教学法

直接教学法

陈　娅

1. 直接教学法的定义

所谓直接教学法(The Direct Method)，就是直接用外语教外语，不用学生的母语，不用翻译，也不注重形式语法。它的教学目标不是规范的书面语，而是外语口语。直接法主张采用口语材料作为教学内容，广泛利用手势、动作、表情、实物、图画等直观手段，强调模仿，主张用教儿童学习本族语言的方法，“通过说话学说话”的方法来学习外语。教学过程是一句一句地听、模仿、反复练习，直到养成语言习惯。直接法在教活语言，特别是在培养口语能力方面，取得了显著的成绩。

直接教学法提倡在教室中直接以第二语言或目标语(target language)来沟通或教学。传统的语法翻译法(The Grammar-Translation Method)往往过度强调母语在第二语言学习中的重要性，并且过于强调语法知识的记忆。在这样的学习方式下，学生常常无法有效地运用所学的词汇或语法知识来沟通。直接教学法特别针对语法翻译法的缺点，从一开始就很重视学生听说沟通能力的培养，拒绝填鸭式的语法规则教学，强调语言的自然学习。因此，本教学法又叫做 Anti-grammatical Method。它包含三个方面的意思：直接学习、直接理解和直接应用。

2. 历史与背景

直接法产生于改革的实践，但改革是社会需要引发的。在 19 世纪 70—80 年代，欧洲资本主义的发展导致贸易的活跃、殖民地的争夺以及各国决策的变动，从而引起了在广泛范围内使用外语直接交际的需要。从拉丁语教学沿袭下来的翻译法再也满足不了这种需要。加之心理学和教育学研究了学生的年龄特征、兴趣、动机；普通语言学开始了描写性的研究，明确了语言的声音本质、音符之间的关系、词的组合和多义。据此，人们发现不同语言之间在结构和词汇上并不等值；逐词翻译显然不能作为外语教学法的基础。这些相关学科的发展都为直接教学法的形成提供了理论基础。直接教学法是从自然教学法发展起来的。1892 年德国政府下令推行改革法，1901 年法国教育部将其定名为直接法。

所以，直接法虽与自然教学法采用相同的基本原理——语言是一套习惯，语言活动是感觉和记忆而非思维，应按学习母语的心理、生理规则学习外语，但得出了不尽相同的教学法结论：外语学习应该通过口语活动学习有联系的整体。故直接法主张句单位教学。它认为翻译法既浪费时间，又妨碍外语气氛的形成，且易使学生按照本族语去类推外语句子，故应尽量排除，而应建立外语词语与实际的直接联系，以培养学生使用外语思维。因此，必须重视听觉感知和听觉记忆。这样，它把语言教学提到了前所未有的重要地位，并因而要求先听说后读写，要求模仿和用外语类推。

3. 在外校的运用

外语学校的教学模式基本为全外语教学(教师使用外语进行教学，并广泛使用实物、图画、手势、表情等直观手段对外语的词义和句子做解释)，模仿、朗读和问答是主要的教学活动形式(这些活动有利于帮助学生掌握好正确的语音、语调和培养口头表达能力)，教师要求学生在提问或对教师的问题做回答时，均以完整的句子说出问句或答句。因此，在外语学校的教学过程中，直接教学法被广泛运用。特别是在对《看听学》教材的使用过程中，更加凸显了它的直观性和有效性。我们要求学生能对照教材中的图片来模仿范例句型，从而养成语言习惯。尤其是在谈论“天气”、“问路”、“实物描述”、“比较级”等话题时运用得更为广泛。

例如，我校孙宇敏老师在谈论“天气”这一话题时，不断要求学生用“What's the weather like today?”和“How is the weather today?”来提问，从而使学生熟记了句型。但是，教师并没有阐述这两个问句是如何构成的。另外，在对于有关天气的单词教学中，教师并没有仅以“单词表”(discrete vocabulary list)的方式呈现词汇，而是尽量将单词呈现在有意义的句子中。这样，学生才能将单词的自然使用情境一并记在脑海中。

又如，我校余静老师在讲述比较级的时候运用了大量的图片来对比和比较，然后通过对句型的不断操练让学生熟悉句型。接下来，她又结合图片给学生介绍了房屋及其各个部分的名称，从而让学生有了更为直观的印象。

在教学实践中我们一般遵循以下几个原则：

第一，课堂中禁用母语。母语学习者因为没有其他语言的干扰，母语的学习才能如此成功。因此，直接教学法的支持者认为第二语言的学习也应将学生其他语言(母语)的干扰减到最低。教师不用母语来解释、翻译或分析。

例如，我校陈娅老师在讲述“lifelike”这个词的时候，给学生展示了蜡像和真人的合影图片。并通过猜测哪个是真人的活动来激起学生的好奇心，从而引出了“lifelike（栩栩如生的）”这个生词，以这种直观感知的方式加深了学生的印象。

第二，就语法而言，外语学习应避免语法规则的解释或记忆。因为在母语的学习环境中即使不特别去记忆或是分析语法规则，也能从单纯的自然接触中习得母语的语法规则。因此，在学习第二语言时，教师可以通过提供大量的范例和语料让学生自然而然从每天所接触的语料资讯中直接归纳出语法。在学生有疑问时，教师尽量以示范代替解释或翻译。这意味着教师要有极佳的创意、丰富的想象力、表达能力以及形象的肢体语言。

第三，本教学法对单词的重视远远胜过语法。在单词教学时，教师不会仅以“单词表”的方式呈现词汇，而会尽量将单词呈现在有意义的句子或段落中。这样，学生才能将单词的自然使用情境一并记在脑海中。教师应随时注意学生是否能正确地把单词应用在完整的句子中。

例如，我校蔡文静老师在介绍副词时，先从对图片的描述由形容词的使用自然地过渡到了副词的使用。然后运用大量的图片和丰富的肢体语言来操练副词在句中的位置和用法。但是在教学的全过程中并没有去强调在语法上它们有什么异同，而是在学生犯错误的时候去纠正他们，让他们形成正确的语言习惯。

第四，当学生犯错的时候，如果学生自己没有察觉错误或不知如何改正时，教师应立即给学生提供正确答案。教师直接更正时，要尽量不只是针对犯错的学生，而是带着全班针对错误处做练习。如果是让学生自行改正，教师可以应用以下技巧来明示学生的错误：提高错误处的语调；重复学生的句子，但是在错误处之前停下来；让学生在正确答案和所犯错误间做选择。

4. 优点与不足

直接教学法采用各种直观教具，广泛运用接近实际生活的教学方式，有助于培养学习者用外语思维的能力。强调直接学习的直接应用，注重语言实践练习，学生学习积极性高，学习兴趣浓厚。重视口语和语音教学，能有效地培养学生的语言运用能力。直接法比起古典语法翻译法是教学法史上的一大进步，成为以后的听说法、视听法、功能法等现代改革派的开端，但它完全是针对语法翻译法的弊端提出的，本身难免有局限性和片面性，在教学中偏重经验、感性认识，而对学生的文学修养不够注意，导致学生对许多语言现象只知其然而不知其所以然。其缺点之一便是教师可能会缺乏一套系统的方式来介绍语法，因此，造成学生对一些抽象和复杂的概念难以理解。另外，它本身缺乏明晰的语法解释，导致学生说出的话语法错误较多。就教学程序而言，本教学法强调书写的教学应在听写能力之后。但是，现今已有许多语言研究证明，学习新词汇时，若能同时教单词的发音及其书写，将更能加深学习者的记忆深度。因此，听、说、读、写能力的培养是否应该“循序渐进”仍然是一个未定的议题。

Teaching Plan of *Look Listen and Learn* Book Ⅱ Lesson 81-82

教师：蔡文静

Teaching Aims:

1. To get the students to know how to use adverbs.
2. To get the students to practice how to ask a question and get the answer.
3. To get the students to know how to make an article more beautiful.

Teaching Objects:

The students in Class Eight, Junior Two.

Language Points:

1. The spelling of the adverbs.
2. The using of the adverbs.

Teaching Aids:

Multi-media teaching aid.

Teaching Methods:

1. Audio-visual Method.
2. Communicative Approach.
3. Task-based Approach.

Teaching Procedures

	First, review some important activities our students attended last year. Ask questions and teach the students how to answer by using adverbs. Q: How were their posters? A: They were beautiful / creative. Q: How did they design the posters? A: They designed them beautifully / creatively.

How were their posters?

How did they design the posters?

They were beautiful / creative.

They designed them beautifully / creatively.

Activate

在课堂教学开始前的较短时间内灵活安排新颖的导入活动，促使全班学生集中注意力，迅速进入学习状态。

Second, let the students know more about the adverbs by practising.

Example:

Q: How was their handwriting?

A: They were beautiful.

Q: How did they write?

A: They wrote beautifully.

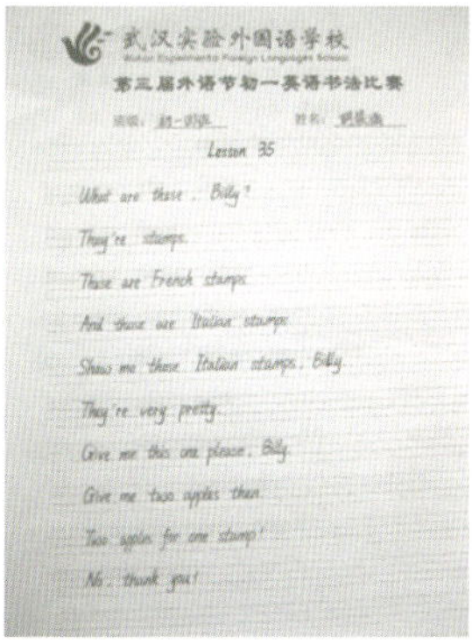
武汉实验外国语学校

第三届外语节初一英语书法比赛

Lesson 35

What are these, Billy?

They're stamps.

These are French stamps.

And those are Italian stamps.

Show me those Italian stamps, Billy.

They're very pretty.

Give me this one please, Billy.

Give me two apples then.

Two apples for one stamp!

No, thank you!

They wrote beautifully.

How did they write?

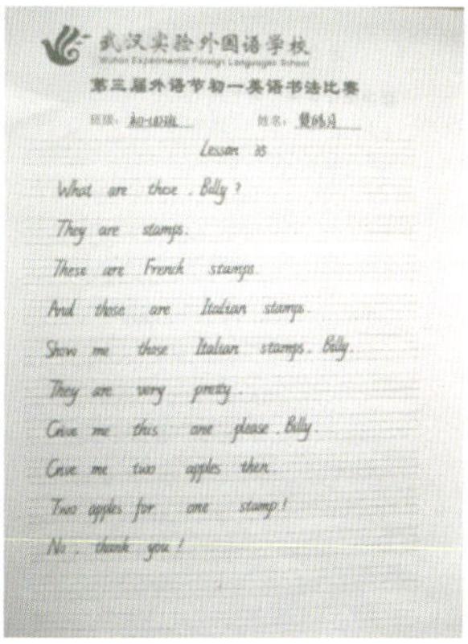
武汉实验外国语学校

第三届外语节初一英语书法比赛

Lesson 35

What are these, Billy?

They are stamps.

These are French stamps.

And those are Italian stamps.

Show me those Italian stamps, Billy.

They are very pretty.

Give me this one please, Billy.

Give me two apples then.

Two apples for one stamp!

No, thank you!

	 Foreign Languages Culture Festival Ceremony They spoke fluent English. How did they speak English? They spoke English fluently.  How did they dance? They danced well. 
***B*uild** 运用综合教学方法指导教学设计，营造良好的学习氛围，使学生快乐、自然、轻松、有效地学习语言。	Third, practice the drill by looking at the pictures on the screen. Q：How did she jump? A：She jumped high.  How did she jump? She jumped high.   How did he jump? He jumped far.  How did they run? They ran fast / quickly.  How did they cheer? They cheered happily.

Do the pair work by using the pictures on the screen pair by pair.

Example:

Q: How did the sun shine yesterday?

A: The sun shone warmly yesterday.

yesterday

Example: How did the sun shine yesterday?

The sun shone warmly yesterday.

yesterday afternoon

How did it rain yesterday afternoon?

It rained heavily yesterday afternoon.

the other day

How did it drink the other day?

It drank thirstily the other day.

last night

How did they sing last night?

They sang softly last night.

the day before yesterday

How did she eat the day before yesterday?

She ate hungrily the day before yesterday.

last Friday

How did the driver drive last Friday?

He drove dangerously last Friday.

	 a moment ago How did he shout a moment ago? He shouted angrily a moment ago.  an hour ago How did he ride a horse an hour ago? He rode quickly an hour ago.  during play time How did they play during play time? They played happily during play time.  yesterday evening How did he dance yesterday evening? He danced funnily yesterday evening.
Cultivate 按照启发式教学原则，设计饶有趣味的训练来充分调动学生学习的主动性。	Listen and repeat each sentence. Then let the students know the meanings of the new words and expressions. While other students are listening to the tape, he/she will listen to a loud song prepared by the teacher. Then he/ she may try to get the missing words by asking you the questions: Example: Q: How did it rain the other day? A: It rained heavily the other day. **Lesson 81 Sue's diary: A day indoors** The other day it rained__heavily__, so we stayed indoors. We made a puppet. We used a sheet of paper, some large corks and some string. We worked __busily__ for two hours. At last the puppet was ready. We painted his face__carefully__. Then Sandy pulled the strings and our puppet danced. He danced__very well__.

Listen again. Listen and repeat each sentence after the tape. Let the students know the meaning of the new words by showing the pictures.

Lesson 81 Sue's diary: A day indoors

The other day it rained heavily, so we stayed indoors.

We made a **puppet**.

We used a sheet of paper, some large **corks** and some **string**.

We worked busily for two hours.

At last the puppet was ready.

We **painted** his face carefully.

Then Sandy pulled the strings and our puppet danced.

He danced very well.

Develop

设计真实的语言环境来综合概括构建及养成部分所传达的语言信息，巩固课堂教学、衔接新旧知识、贯通前后内容，帮助学生学习训练，复习巩固。

Ask the students why people use adverbs and have a small discussion. Then, give the students a passage with some blanks. Ask the students to use the adverbs to make this passage beautiful.

Can you use the things we learn today to make this passage beautiful?

Last week I went to the theatre. I had a very good seat. The play was very interesting. I did not enjoy it. A young man and a young woman were sitting behind me. They were talking __loudly__. I got very angry. I could not hear the actors. I turned round. I looked at the man and the woman __angrily__. They did not pay any attention. In the end, I could not bear it. I turned round again. "I can't hear a word!" I said __angrily__.

"It's none of your business," the young man said __rudely__. "This is a private conversation!"

Evaluate

评估教学活动的实际效果，分析学习成效，帮助学生排除学习障碍。

Evaluation Activity

Review the adverbs we've learned in this class and then ask the students to play a guessing game about the adverbs. This activity helps us to evaluate how well the students grasp the language points we've learned.

Rules：
1. Work in a group of 4-5.
2. One of the group members may stand in front of the class and face the group members.
3. Other students may look at the screen and explain the words you see.
4. You can't mention the words on the screen. You have only one chance to say "pass" to get the next word.
5. Each group has only 30 seconds. The group which gets the most words with the shortest time is the winner.

By doing this activity, I found that most students have already grasped the using of some simple adverbs. But they still have some problems with the words like "hard" and "hardly".

Homework

1. Recite Lesson 81.
2. Workbook Lesson 81 & 82.

课程设计及反思

教师：蔡文静

我的这节课选取了上海外语教育出版社出版的《看听学》系列教材学生用书第二册的第81课Sue's diary：A day indoors和第82课句型练习课。这是一节听说课。

我这节课的教学目的是让学生初步接触副词，了解副词的基本构成以及副词修饰动词的作用并掌握其用法。在这一节课里，我主要使用了直接教学法、视听法以及游戏教学法。

第一步：Activate 激活

在本环节中，我选取了同学们这一年来在学校经历过的几件大事，如：外语文化节颁奖典礼、运动会等的图片和视频，首先让学生就这些他们熟悉而又感兴趣的话题进行讨论，通过讨论引出新的语言项目，让学生在不知不觉中接触并掌握新的语言表达方式。这个环节的设计体现了自然教学法和听说教学法的应用，即首先自然进入，层层推进，让学生自然地进入语言学习。其中我还使用了视听教学法，播放了两段视频，分别体现出两个动作的程度，从而引出两个副词。在这里应用多媒体技术便于创设情景，激发兴趣。它以新颖的形式、丰富的内容、声型兼备、动静结合的方式全方位地刺激学生的感官，形象生动地显示了教学内容，调动了有意注意，培养了学生的学习兴趣和形象思维能力。

第二步：Build 构建

在句型练习阶段，我主要使用了直接教学法。具体步骤如下：首先让学生回顾刚刚接触和学习的句型和副词的组成方法。然后给出图片，请同学们用所学句型和知识按照每幅图片所体现出的内容进行句型操练。这个环节的设计体现出了直接教学法的几个原则：1. 建立语言与外界经验的联系，从而使语言同它所代表的事物或意义直接联系，避免经过母语翻译；2. 以口语训练为基础；3. 句本位原则，使学生既学到了单词又学到了语法；4. 通过模仿重复所学句子，形成深刻的语言习惯。

第三步：Cultivate 养成

在进入课文环节时，我主要使用了听说教学法。具体的步骤如下：1. 关书听，掌握文章大意；2. 关书听，让学生找到所需的重要信息；3. 开书听，模仿每一句的语音语调；4. 开书听，将模仿任务落实到每个学生。通过听说教学法的运用，让学生形成最地道的语音、语调和语言习惯。让重复变成习惯，让习惯帮助语言的形成。

第四步：Develop 发展

在本环节中，我让学生在所学内容的基础上思考人们为什么要使用副词，副词的作用是什么。从而使学生能更好地理解副词的意义。然后，给学生一篇文章，我将文章中原有的副词全部抽出，让学生运用所学副词将文章美化。

第五步：Evaluate 评价

在活动环节中，我使用了游戏教学法。我让学生回顾了本节课所学的副词后，设计了一个猜字游戏：将学生分组，每组选派一位同学轮流上台背对屏幕，然后每个小组的其他成员对屏幕上闪现出来的副词进行描述，他们可以使用语言描述或是身体动作来提示台上的同学。这个方法的运用收到了两个良好的效果：一是小组竞争最大限度地调动了学生参与的积极性。二是通过游戏检测学生对本节课所学内容的掌握情况。

Teaching Plan of *An Integrated English Course* Book 4 Unit 6 Item 3

教师：陈娅

Teaching Aims:

1. To enable the students to get the general information of Madame Tussaud's.
2. Make the students understand how to introduce a place like Madame Tussaud's.
3. To enable the students to do some target listening and reading exercises.

Teaching Objects:

Students in Class Three, Junior Three, Wuhan Experimental Foreign Languages School.

Language Points:

1. The description of Madame Tussaud's.
2. Some adjectives for describing things.

Teaching Aids:

Multimedia, radio, blackboard and some listening and reading materials.

Teaching Methods:

1. Functional Approach (to make the students know the aim of the lesson is to search for information through listening and reading).
2. Communicative Approach (including question-answer-discussion).
3. CAI (Computer-Assisted Instruction) Teaching Approach.

Teaching Procedures

Activate

在课堂教学开始前的较短时间内灵活安排新颖的导入活动，促使全班学生集中注意力，迅速进入学习状态。

1. Duty report.

One student gives an English duty report.

2. A guessing game to lead in the topic “Madame Tussaud’s”.

T：At the beginning of the class, let’s play a guessing game. I want to know how much you know about me. Now I’ll give you some sentences about my personal experiences, and you should judge if they are true or false. If you are right, you can go on guessing. But if you are wrong, you should quit.

Ask the students to do some T or F questions about the teacher’s personal experiences. The “True of False” sentences are：

(1) I’ve been to London. (T)

(2) I lived in Oxford for three weeks. (F)

It should be “I lived in Cambridge for three weeks.”

(3) I’ve visited London Eye and also had a ride on it. (T)

(4) I went to London in 2007. (T)

(5) I met Jonny Depp and took a photo with him. (F)

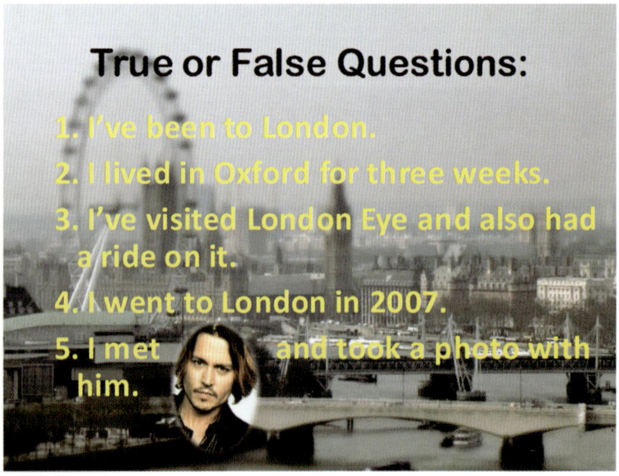

The teacher shows the students a picture to prove that she’s just met the waxwork of Jonny Depp and took a photo with it.

	T：What is this "Jonny Depp" made of? Yes, it is not a real person. It is made of wax. So it is a waxwork, and it is in a waxwork museum in London. We call this museum "Madame Tussaud's". 
***B*uild** 运用综合教学方法指导教学设计，营造良好的学习氛围，使学生快乐、自然、轻松、有效地学习语言。	And then elicit the topic "Madame Tussaud's". 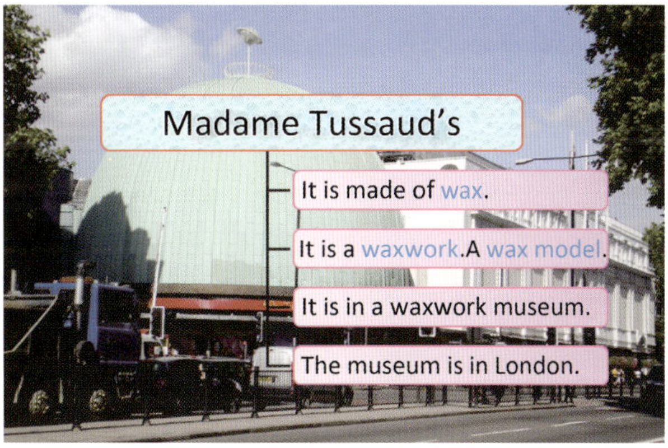 Then the teacher shows some pictures of real persons and their wax models, and asks the students to compare. T：Can you tell which one is the real person if the real person and the wax model stand together? Here are some pictures for you to judge. Ask the students to identify the real person according to some photos. And then elicit the new word "lifelike".

<table>
<tr><td></td><td>

New words:
① lifelike adj.: being a very close or exact representation
e.g.: The digital camera can provide more lifelike photos.</td></tr>
<tr><td>Cultivate

按照启发式教学原则，设计饶有趣味的训练来充分调动学生学习的主动性。</td><td>3. Brief introduction of the wax models in Madame Tussaud's.
T: What kind of people should be in Madame Tussaud's?
S: Some famous people (celebrities).
T: Can you give me some examples? I can show you one first. For example, I think Bruce Lee should be in Madame Tussaud's, because he is so famous for his Chinese Kungfu. And I think he is the father of Chinese Kungfu. So he should be inside. Now discuss with your classmates and give me your ideas.

</td></tr>
</table>

	Students' discussion about "Who should be in Madame Tussaud's?" Ask some students to speak out their opinions. They should begin like this: S: I think ... should be in Madame Tussaud's. Because he/she ... The teacher gives a conclusion about the celebrities in Madame Tussaud's, just like "characters from the movie", "sport stars", "royalty", etc., and meanwhile elicits the new words "politician", "pop idol".  

New words:

① politician *n.*: person actively (and usually professionally) concerned with politics

② idol *n.*: sb. or sth. admired or loved too much

4. The text.

T: There is a passage which is about the brief introduction of Madame Tussaud's in our book. Please listen and finish Exercise One.

Firstly, ask the students to listen to the tape and finish Exercise One in their books. Secondly, ask the students to read the text and then finish Exercise Two.

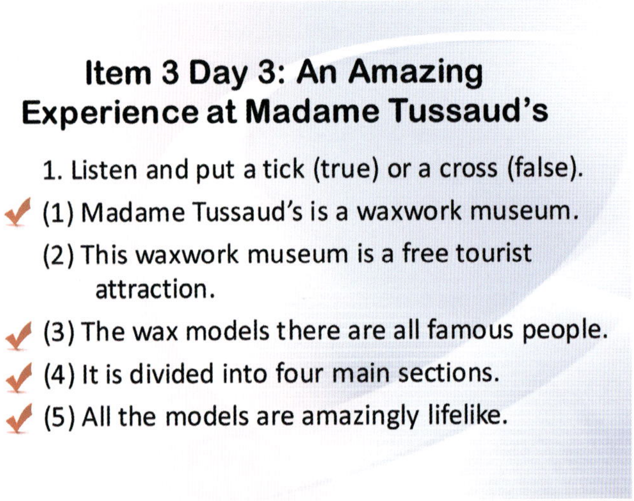

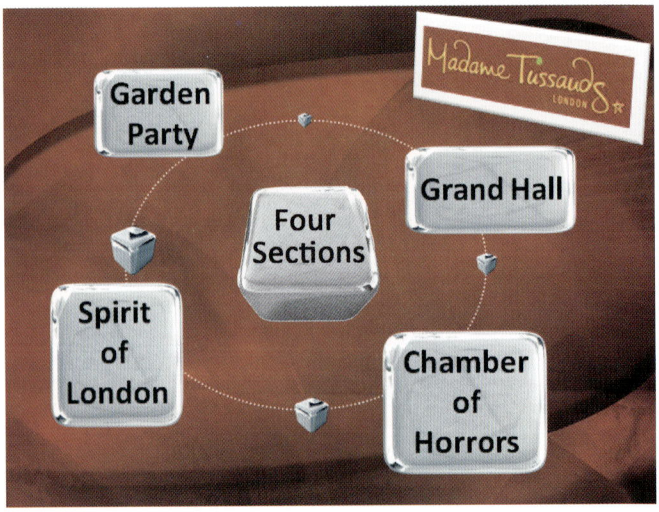

<table>
<tr>
<td></td>
<td>
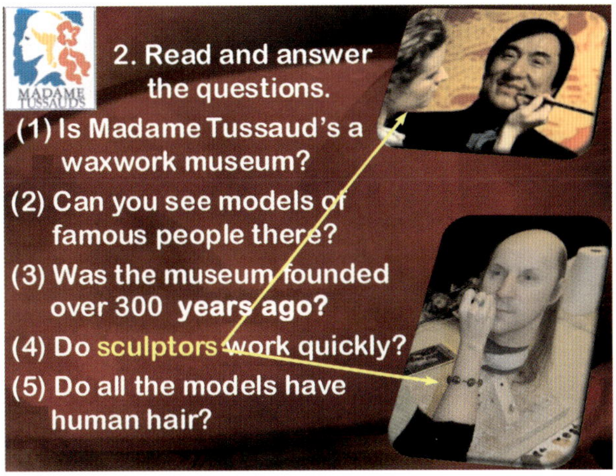

The students read after the tape together. The teacher should ask the students some questions and also explain some new words to make sure that they understand the text.
New words:
① sculptor *n.*: someone who makes sculptures
② infamous *adj.*: well-known for being bad
e.g.: Hitler is one of the infamous people in the world.
③ chamber *n.*: room or a room set aside for special purpose
</td>
</tr>
<tr>
<td>
Develop
设计真实的语言环境来综合概括构建及养成部分所传达的语言信息，巩固课堂教学、衔接新旧知识、贯通前后内容，帮助学生学习训练，复习巩固。
</td>
<td>
5. Listening practice for further understanding.
T: Do you want to know some more information about Madame Tussaud's? There is a video about it. Let's watch it together and try to catch some more details.
Let the students watch a video about Madame Tussaud's and ask them to catch some more details about it.
Questions: How old is Madame Tussaud's? How many wax models are there? How many tourists are there each year? How can we buy the tickets?
Then ask the students to think about some words that can describe Madame Tussaud's, and then find out some adjectives according to a listening material of the tourists' feedback. (Show the students the listening material.)
</td>
</tr>
</table>

Transcript:

—I'm from Hunan. It's terrific and fabulous. It really looks like real people and I have just great fun here.

—I love it because you can make photos with lots of famous persons (I love it because you can take photos with lots of famous people).

—A really good and really interesting experience.

—It's a good place.

—It's awesome.

6. Reading comprehension for further understanding.

T: Do you want to go to Madame Tussaud's one day? Where can you get some information if you will go to visit Madame Tussaud's? Just like how to get there? What is the price? The best way to get information is surfing the Internet. I've already downloaded some pictures from the official website of Madame Tussaud's. And now you will do some reading comprehension. You can finish them according to the pictures shown on the screen.

Hand out a piece of paper to each student with some reading exercises on it (see the appendix). And then ask the students to finish the exercises according to the pictures shown on the screen.

Then check the answers together.

(1) Where can we visit Madame Tussaud's in China?

(2) How many museums of Madame Tussaud's are there in the USA?

Getting Here

Our Address

Madame Tussauds, Marylebone Road, London NW1 5LR

By Tube

Madame Tussauds is a two minute walk from Baker Street tube station. Baker Street underground station is on the Bakerloo, Circle, Jubilee, Metropolitan and Hammersmith & City lines, making it a short, easy journey from anywhere on the central London tube network.

By Train

Marylebone Station is within 10 minutes walking distance of Madame Tussauds. Euston, St.Pancras, Paddington, Victoria, Waterloo and Charing Cross mainline stations are all within five stops on the tube.

By Bus

The following bus numbers travel to Madame Tussauds: 13, 18, 27, 30, 74, 82, 113, 139, 189, 205, 274 and 453.

Bus information from Transport for London

By Coach

There is a coach drop off and pick up point situated on Marylebone Road.

By Car

Marylebone Road is an extension of the A40, one of the major routes in and out of London. Marylebone Road joins up with the Euston Road which passes by Kings Cross.

Our Address

(3) How can you get to Madame Tussaud's in London?

(4) Is it convenient for you to park your car near Madame Tussaud's? Why?

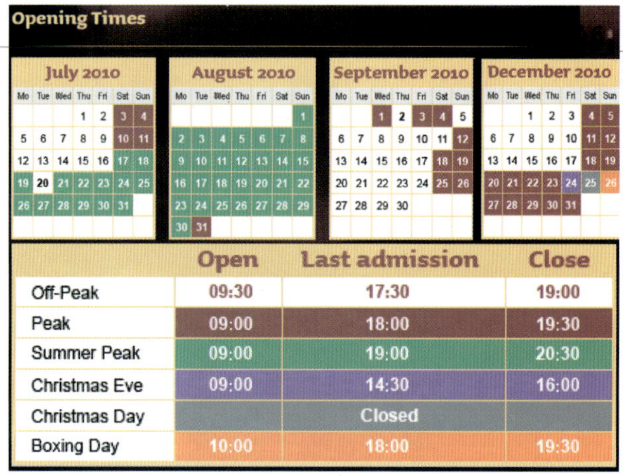

(   ) (5) When can you enter Madame Tussaud's on December 24th?

A. 9: 00 a. m.   B. 4: 00 p. m.   C. 6: 00 p. m.

(   ) (6) It has more tourists in ________.

A. July   B. August   C. December

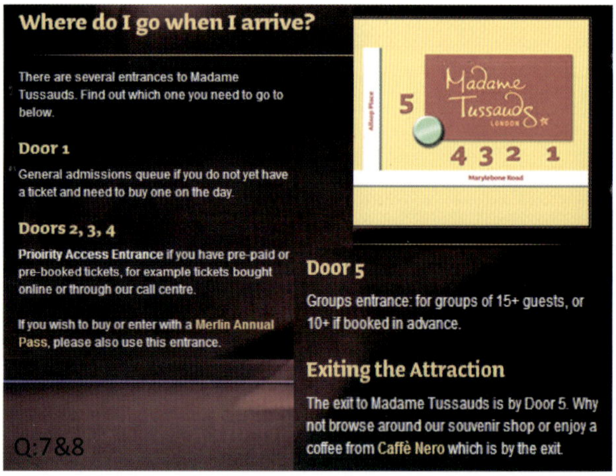

(   ) (7) If you've bought tickets online or through the call centre, from which door can you get into Madame Tussaud's?

A. Door 1.   B. Door 3.   C. Door 5.

(   ) (8) If you want to buy some souvenirs, you'd better go through ________.

A. Door 2   B. Door 4   C. Door 5

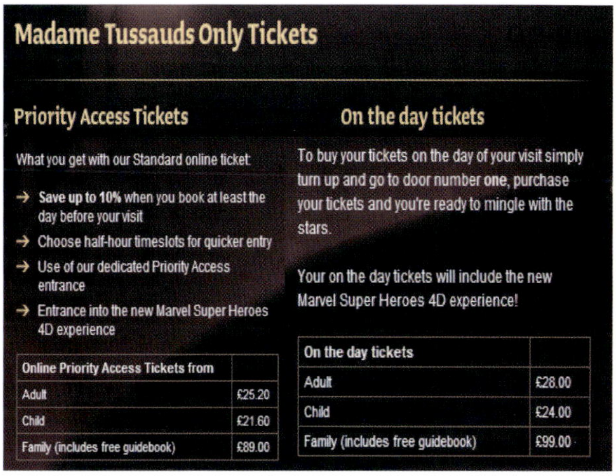

Madame Tussauds Only Tickets

Priority Access Tickets

What you get with our Standard online ticket:

- Save up to 10% when you book at least the day before your visit
- Choose half-hour timeslots for quicker entry
- Use of our dedicated Priority Access entrance
- Entrance into the new Marvel Super Heroes 4D experience

Online Priority Access Tickets from	
Adult	£25.20
Child	£21.60
Family (includes free guidebook)	£89.00

On the day tickets

To buy your tickets on the day of your visit simply turn up and go to door number one, purchase your tickets and you're ready to mingle with the stars.

Your on the day tickets will include the new Marvel Super Heroes 4D experience!

On the day tickets	
Adult	£28.00
Child	£24.00
Family (includes free guidebook)	£99.00

True or False:

( ) (9) If you book a ticket online in advance, the ticket will be more expensive.

( ) (10) You can get the free guidebook if you buy family tickets.

7. Development.

T: If we will set up a museum of Madame Tussaud's in Wuhan. Can you give me some ideas? Where shall we build it? Who should be inside? How much is the ticket?

Then ask the students to discuss with their classmates, and give a presentation on how to set up a Madame Tussaud's in Wuhan.

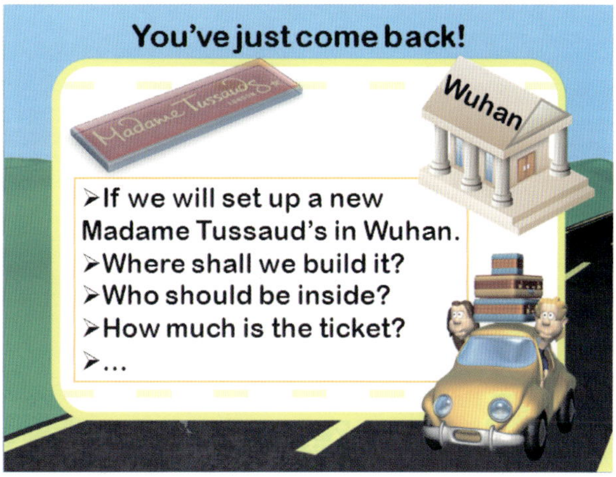

Evaluate 评估教学活动的实际效果，分析学习成效，帮助学生排除学习障碍。	**8. Homework.** Finish Exercise 4 on P112 and read this item fluently.

Notes:

Answers:

1. We can visit Madame Tussaud's in Hong Kong and Shanghai in China.
2. There are four museums of Madame Tussaud's in the USA.
3. We can get to Madame Tussaud's by tube, by train, by bus, by coach and by car.
4. Yes, it is. Because there are many car parks near Madame Tussaud's.

5. A　6. B　7. B　8. C　9. F　10. T

课程设计及反思

教师：陈娅

我的这节课选取了《英语综合教程》第四册第六单元的 Item 3，是一节阅读课。这节课的教学目的是以这篇阅读为载体，通过相关资料的补充使学生在听、说、读三个方面都能有所涉及，进一步培养学生的阅读能力。我使用了直接法和任务型教学法等。具体步骤如下：

第一步：激活(Activate)

我通过一个关于对我本人在伦敦旅游的猜谜游戏开始了我的课堂导入。其目的是通过全员参与，吸引所有学生的注意力，从而进入主题“杜莎夫人蜡像馆”。

第二步：构建(Build)

在学生初步接触蜡像馆这个主题后，我运用了直接教学法。我展示了蜡像与真人的合影，并让学生猜测哪个是真人。其目的是给学生一个直观的印象“蜡像馆里面的人究竟是怎样的”，另一个目的是引导出生词“lifelike”(栩栩如生的)。事实证明，直接的图片对比更能让学生理解并记住生词。

第三步：养成(Cultivate)

接下来我给了学生一个任务，要求他们讨论“谁应该被做成模特放在蜡像馆里”。学生既给出他们的人选，同样也要阐述理由。这样在口语方面也能做到相关的操练。在听完学生的观点后我以图片的方式来总结，介绍蜡像馆里的主要人物分类。

接下来就是常规的课文部分的听读练习和讲解。通过听读操练和完成课本中的练习使课堂内容回归到课本知识，并对里面的生词和句型做适当的讲解。然后要求学生跟读课文。

第四步：发展(Develop)

在接下来的拓展练习中，我采用了视听法和任务型教学法，给学生播放了一段关于介绍蜡像馆的视频。在看和听的同时，我要求学生去获取一些细节的信息。这一任务的目的是要告诉学生，尽管不能看懂全部视频，但还是能获取一些有用的信息。为了能进一步让学生知道如何发表自己的观点，我播放了一段关于游客反馈的音频。一方面让学生从听力练习中获取更多的细节知识，另一方面让他们掌握一些他们可以用到的形容词。

在阅读能力的训练方面，我采用了任务型教学法。我事先从蜡像馆的官方网站上截取了一些有关蜡像馆游览的图片信息，并以阅读理解的形式展现出来。这一步骤的任务是让学生在快速阅读中去搜索有用的信息。

第五步：评价(Evaluate)

在最后的拓展练习部分，我希望能对学生进行一定的情感教育。于是我使用了任务型教学法，给学生设定了任务："设想我们会在家乡武汉建一个蜡像馆，同学们会有些什么想法呢?"要求学生通过讨论就蜡像馆的选址、模特和票价等相关信息做一个简短的报告。大部分学生都能将想法有条理地表达出来。

☞ 教学反思：

在课程的设置方面，我用游戏作为导入来激发学生的求知欲，起到了很好的效果。在听力和阅读能力培养方面，我充分利用网络上的资源，下载了视频简介和官网上的图片，并自行设计了阅读训练题，使得整节课容量大、节奏快。学生获取了很多课本上没有的知识，拓宽了视野，同时也训练了听力和阅读。课堂从始至终贯穿了知识与能力并重的特点，将课本知识与应试训练有机地结合起来。在最后的拓展练习中，我以"如何在武汉建立一个蜡像馆"作为话题让学生展开讨论，将情感意识也贯穿到课堂内容中。但这一环节没能做完，因为前面的容量过大。如果还想有所改进的话，我觉得可以设置一些以学生自主学习探究为主的课堂教学模式，例如学生互相出题、互相提问等。我认为，对于既要上新课又要备考的初三学生来说，这种类型的英语课堂教学是有借鉴意义的。

Teaching Plan of *An Intergrated English Course* Book 1 Unit 8 Weather Getting Started & Dialogue 1

教师：孙宇敏

Teaching Aims:

1. To get the students to know the new words about all kinds of weather.
2. To get the students to describe how people feel and what people can do on the days of different weather.

Teaching Objects:

Junior One students of Wuhan Foreign Languages School.

Language Points:

1. Get the students to know how to express the weather and the temperature.
   How is the weather? /What is the weather like?
   It's rainy/It has drizzle/moderate rain/heavy rain, etc.
   What is the temperature?
   It's 3 degrees to 8 degrees centigrade. (3℃-8℃) / The temperature is 3 degrees with a high of 8 degrees.
2. Direct students to talk about weather and the suitable activities to do.

Teaching Aids:

Multi-media, students' book, and blackboard.

Teaching Methods:

1. Task-based Language Teaching Approach.
2. Direct Method Language Teaching Approach.

Teaching Procedures	
***A**ctivate* 在课堂教学开始前的较短时间内灵活安排新颖的导入活动，促使全班学生集中注意力，迅速进入学习状态。	Ask the students how they feel and lead them to think of the ways of expressing different weather. Let the students draw different signs of weather and let all of them judge which one draws the best. And offer the winner a small present.  How do you feel, cold or warm? I feel cold.
***B**uild* 运用综合教学方法指导教学设计，营造良好的学习氛围，使学生快乐、自然、轻松、有效地学习语言。	Present the students the exact signs of different weather and guide them to practice the sentence patterns (introduce the new words by offering the pictures): —How is the weather? /What is the weather like? —It's rainy/It has drizzle/moderate rain/heavy rain, etc.   What's the weather like today? How is the weather? It's rainy.

Snow
light snow
moderate snow
heavy snow

Rain
drizzle
moderate rain
heavy rain

snowstorm
hail
cloudless
XINHUAN
thunderstorm
after the storm

Then ask the students if they get used to it and let them know how to describe the temperature.

—What is the temperature?

—It's 3 degrees to 8 degrees centigrade. （3℃-8℃） / The temperature is 3 degrees with a high of 8 degrees.

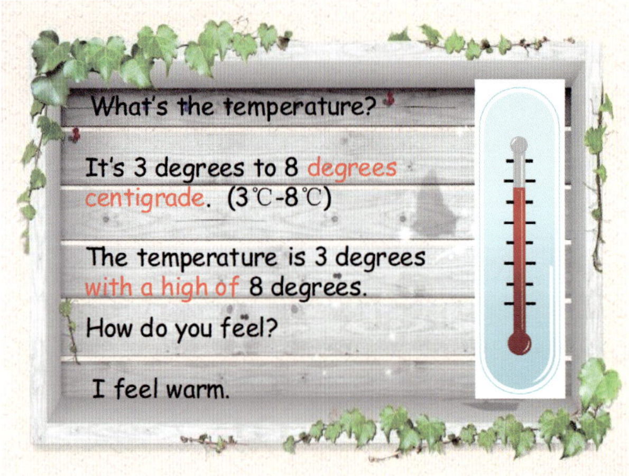

Offer different pictures of the weather and people, let the students practice the sentence patterns they've just learned and ask how people feel.

Then let the students think about what we will do if we meet different weather.

—If it is rainy, I will go to the movies.

snowy
-6 ℃ -0 ℃

windy/rainy
16 ℃ -20 ℃

foggy
5 ℃ -8 ℃

freezing

terrible

awful

If it's …, I will…
If it's rainy, I will go to the movies.

hiking

relax on the beach

stay at home

have a picnic

make a snowman

Cultivate

按照启发式教学原则，设计饶有趣味的训练来充分调动学生学习的主动性。

Listen and ask. Let the students listen to the tape and answer the following questions. (New words: freezing, get used to)

—What is the weather like today?

—How does she feel?

—What is the weather going to be like this weekend?

—What will she do if she doesn't get used to the weather here?

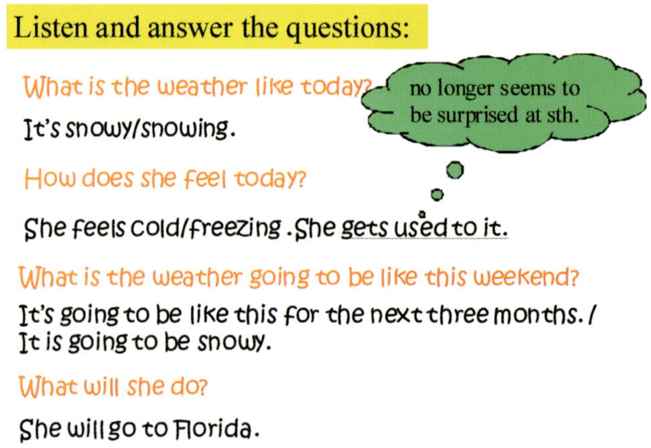

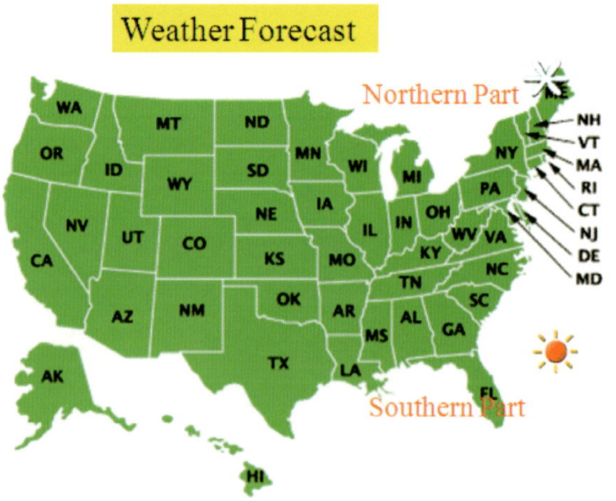

Then group reading and individual reading.

Develop

设计真实的语言环境来综合概括构建及养成部分所传达的语言信息，巩固课堂教学、衔接新旧知识、贯通前后内容，帮助学生学习训练，复习巩固。

Let the students do group work. Offer the weather forecast of China on May Day to the students, and ask them to make dialogues of how the weather will be, where they will go to spend the holiday and what they will do.

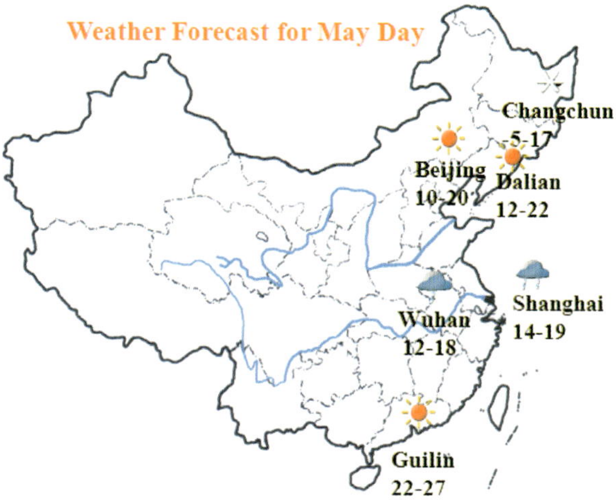

Then ask if the students can imagine a day in the future, how the weather will be and what people can do at that time.

	 Let's imagine: What will the weather be like in the future? What activities can people do at that time? Try to use the sentence patterns you have learned today.
*E*valuate 评估教学活动的实际效果，分析学习成效，帮助学生排除学习障碍。	Assignments：Finish the exercise in the workbook. When I teach the students the new words of the weather，I try to put the words in the sentences but not in the discrete vocabulary list. I offer a lot of pictures and examples so that the students can get the exact language expressions directly and naturally. Then they can use the passive vocabulary in a complete sentence and make a dialogue. After the target dialogue reading，I design a topic，lead them to think what activities people may like doing on the days of different weather. It requires the students to use the target language they have learned during the lesson and communicate in reality. During the lesson，every student has the opportunity to think independently and participate in a group work and even get the sense of accomplishment. Through the participation，experience，interaction，exchange，cooperation in the lesson，the students have learned how to describe different weather and plan the activities.

课程设计及反思

教师：孙宇敏

我这节课选取了《全国外国语学校综合英语》教材第一册第 8 单元 Weather 的 Getting Started 以及 Dialogue 1 部分，是一节精读听说课。

我这节课的教学目的是使学生掌握如何描述各种天气以及气温；谈论在不同天气情况下怎样安排活动。我使用了任务型教学法和直接教学法，以 ABCDE 五步教学模式设计课堂。

具体步骤如下：

激活环节(Activate)：从日常生活入手，与学生寒暄，让学生在黑板上画出他们所见过的或想象的天气图标，并评选出最佳作者并给予奖励。这一环节充分调动了学生的想象力和积极性，在教师的引导下使学生迅速自然地过渡到本课的主题——天气与气温。

构建环节(Build)：根据不同的天气图标，使学生熟悉并练习如何描述天气。接着提供大量的图片和范例，进一步谈论气温，让学生了解并掌握正确的表达。在这个环节，我运用了直接教学法让学生自然而然频繁地接触语料资讯，并从中直接归纳出语言规则。在有关天气的单词教学中，我不是以“单词表”(discrete vocabulary list)的方式呈现词汇，而是尽量把零碎词汇(passive vocabulary)呈现在完整且有意义的句子中，这样，学生才能将单词的自然使用情境一并记在脑海中。在和学生互动的过程中，随时注意学生是否能正确地把单词应用于完整的句子中，为引入正文做好铺垫。在实际教学中，学生运用准确，收到了很好的效果。

养成环节(Cultivate)：在学生了解并掌握了有关天气和温度的表达后，设计新的话题，引导学生思考在不同的天气条件下，可以安排什么活动，从而引入课文。通过听读课文让学生熟悉在特定的情境下如何合理运用句型。这里运用的是任务型教学法，即提出任务，调动他们已有的目的语资源，在实践中感知、认识、应用目的语，在“干”中学，在“用”中学。这样学生在正式听对话前就已经基本掌握对话中的重点单词和句型，并能初步运用。接着通过反复听读与问答，进一步让学生熟悉目的语的习惯表达。这样一堂课的教学目的到这里已经基本呈现，教学重点突出，教学难度层层推进，符合学生的认知规律，能达到很好的效果。在这个环节中，学生练习了听、读，收到了不错的效果。

拓展环节(Develop)：这个环节我采用了任务型教学法，即设计了两个情境，让学生将本课所学的目的语运用到实践中去。能力较弱的学生可以根据第一个假设的场景，运用所学知识达到运用的目的；能力较强的学生也可以发挥想象，在我设计的背景下自行模拟场景进行对话，给了这部分学生更广阔的空间。这样可以照顾到不同层面的学生，让他们都有得说，有得谈。在这个环节中有小组或双人活动，每个人都有自己的任务要完成，在教师的启发下，每个学生都有独立思考、积极参与的机会。教师可以更好地面向全体学生进行教学，易于保持学生学习的积极性，养成良好的学习习惯。

评价环节(Evaluate)：我这节课主要运用了直接教学法以及任务型教学法。顾名思义，直接教学法提倡在教室中直接以第二语言或目标语(target language)来沟通或教学。任务型教学法以任务组织教学，在任务的履行过程中，以参与、体验、互动、交流、合作的学习方式，充分发挥学习者自身的认知能力。这节课有以下特色：

1. 我在这节课中扮演的角色，是学生的伙伴而非权威的指导者，授课中问题的答案由我或者学生来提供。
2. 我重视学生听力、口语沟通能力的培养，强调语言的自然学习，即从单纯的自然接触中，从课堂上的语料资讯中习得目的语的文法规则和表达习惯。
3. 学生通过这堂课的学习，将单词的使用情景化，自然化，存于脑海中，并在课堂中实践运用，当学生犯错时，我及时给出正确答案，使学生印象深刻。
4. 在学生的操练和拓展过程中，我设计的任务梯度层次分明，学生参与面广，最大限度地调动了学生的积极性。在提供任务的过程中使用贴近真实生活的辅助资料，尽量创造真实或接近于真实的环境，让学生尽可能多地接触和加工真实的语言信息，使他们在课堂上使用的语言和技能在实际生活中同样能得到有效的应用。

但是这堂课也有不足之处：

任务设计在形式上可以再丰富一些，除了电视报道，还可以加入旅游指南，在小组活动中可以采取评分或竞赛制进一步调动学生的积极性等。

教学有法，教无定法。今后我将继续学习各种英语教学法，吸取先进的“人性化”教学法最新成果，吸取传统英语教学法中的精华，这有助于我们英语教师在教学中扬长避短，提高自己的教学水平。本课教案及反思仅供大家参考，请指正。

Teaching Plan for *An Integrated English Course* Book Ⅱ Unit 3 A Place to Live

教师：余静

Teaching Aims:

1. Introduce some places where people live and some scenic sports in different parts of the world.
2. Learn to talk about the places where we live and the housing facilities.

Teaching Objects:

Students from Junior 7.

Language Points:

New words: rent, let, advertisement, square meters, bedroom, living-room, dining-room, kitchen, bathroom, bathtub, wash-basin, toilet

Sentence patterns:

A is not as big as B.

They are different in size.

What about...?

Teaching Aids:

Computer and tape-recorder.

Teaching Methods:

The Direct Method.

Teaching Procedures

*A*ctivate 在课堂教学开始前的较短时间内灵活安排新颖的导入活动，促使全班学生集中注意力，迅速进入学习状态。	**Step 1　Duty Report** **Step 2　Revision** Go over the pictures and review the sentence patterns we've learned.  This kitten is the same as that one. They are the same colour. They are of the same colour.  Yao Ming is 2 metres 26 centimetres tall. Mcgrady is 2 metres 3 centimetres tall. They are different in height. Sentence Patterns ■ A and B are the same (size/colour/shape ...). ■ A is the same as B(in size/ colour / shape ...). ■ A and B are of the same (size/colour/shape ...). ■ A is of the same (size/colour/shape ...) as B. ■ A and B are different (in size/colour/shape ...). ■ A is different from B (in size/colour/shape ...).

Step 3 Warming-up

Introduce the places we live and the furnishings.

1. Where do they live?

Where does he live?

the White House

Where does she live?

the Buckingham Palace

Where do they live?

Sydney Opera House

shell

*B*uild

运用综合教学方法指导教学设计，营造良好的学习氛围，使学生快乐、自然、轻松、有效地学习语言。

2. Where do you live? A house or a flat? What parts does it have? What's in each part?

Where do you live, in a flat or in a house?

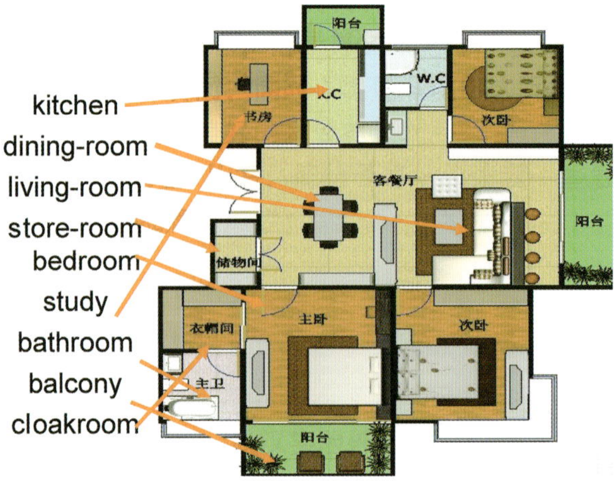

fireplace
armchair
sofa
curtains
coffee-
table
lamp
cushion
carpet

3. Now you don't have your own flat. What can you do? And what kind of flat do you want?

What shall we do if we don't have our own rooms?

rent (v.) a flat → pay money to live in a place and use the things in it

Where can we get the information about the places to rent?

advertisement →

4. Listen and answer.

Listen to D2 and answer the questions:

- *Who wants to rent a flat?*
- *Who is the owner of the flat?*
- *How many bedrooms are there in the flat?*
- *What's in the bathroom?*
- *What is the rent (n.)?*
  (How much should he pay to live here?)
- *How big is it?*

square meters (m^2)

<table>
<tr><td></td><td>Where do you live? Is your flat like this?</td></tr>
<tr><td>

Cultivate

按照启发式教学原则，设计饶有趣味的训练来充分调动学生学习的主动性。

</td><td>

wardrobe bed chair desk

toilet
wash-basin
bathtub
towel
dustbin

refrigerator
oven
cupboard
sink

</td></tr>
</table>

D evelop

设计真实的语言环境来综合概括构建及养成部分所传达的语言信息，巩固课堂教学、衔接新旧知识、贯通前后内容，帮助学生学习训练，复习巩固。

An Activity

Now you are in Shanghai. You want to rent a flat like the one in the following picture.

Make a similar dialogue according to the advertisement.

E valuate

评估教学活动的实际效果，分析学习成效，帮助学生排除学习障碍。

Homework

(1) Recite Dialogue 2.

(2) Finish workbook Exercise 2 and 3.

Teaching Reflection

The students were very interested in talking about their flats, the facilities and some places of interest. But when we began the topic of "renting a flat", they were not so active. I think that's because it's too far away from their life.

课程设计及反思

教师：余静

我选取的是“全国外国语学校英语系列教材”《综合英语教程》初一年级第二学期第三单元的第二个对话，这是一节听说课。

在这节课中我们要学习谈论“我们所居住的地方”——主要是指我们所居住的单元套间内的设施等，学会在生活中怎么去租用一套自己想要的寓所。为了达到这个目的，我采用了多种教学方法：讨论型学习法、听说法，主要采用了直接教学法。

本单元以“房屋·住所·家居”为话题，讨论了生活在城乡的差别、住所里的设施等。本节课是该单元的第二节课，内容主要是吉姆在报纸上看到一份房屋出租广告，于是打电话给房主说想租房，双方谈到租金、套间的各个部分及设施等。这节课的第一个步骤是激活(Activate)环节，包括值日报告和复习。在这个步骤中，我给了学生两幅图片。一幅是两只一样的猫，一幅是运动员姚明和Mcgrady。通过这两幅图来练习句型“be the same as”和“be different from”。培养学生看到实际的东西，然后直接用英语来表达的习惯，直接用英语思维，而不是先想到用汉语表达，再逐字逐句地译成英语。第二个步骤是构建(Build)环节，用英语问题“Do they live in the same place?”来承上启下，通过直接教学法，结合图片，先给学生介绍一些名胜，如the White House，the Buckingham Palace，Sydney Opera House。这样既一目了然，又使人印象深刻。看到了实物，就知道这是what，英语名称就会脱口而出，而不需要用汉语解释：这是白宫，译作the White House。然后我又结合图片给学生介绍房屋及其各个部分以及各个部分的设施，如flat，house，kitchen，bedroom等，直接建立图片中实物与英语单词的联系。如果学生有兴趣的话，还可以介绍一下相关名胜的知识。接着呈现本单元的对话。我先提出问题，引导学生利用所学的知识讨论自己想要的寓所是什么样的，怎样才能找到这样一个寓所。接着我介绍一下吉姆想租房的情况，他想要一个什么样的套间呢？针对对话内容，我设计了6个问题，让学生带着问题去听录音，并做记录。这样，学生听录音的时候就有事可做，听录音的效果比较好。在第三个“养成”(Cultivate)步骤中，为了锻炼学生的口语，我就让他们借助我所提供的图片的帮助，用课堂上所学的内容描述一下自己的住所。最后，在“发展”(Develop)环节中，为了巩固所学知识，我设计了一个活动——“你在上海，去租一间你想要的寓所”。在这个活动中学生能利用所习得的语言知识，解决实际生活中的问题，让学生通过体验、实践、合作、交流来完成任务，在“做中学，用中学”，体会学习的乐趣。

这节课通过利用多种教学法，循序渐进地层层推进，根据教学内容设计任务活动，让学生学会用英语做事，在做事的过程中学习语言，形成综合运用语言的能力。通过这个评估(Evaluate)环节，我感到美中不足的是，“租房”这件事与中学生的实际生活有些差距，在完成最后一项活动时，学生的兴趣不是很大。在今后的教学中，设计任务时要以学生的生活经验和兴趣为出发点，应贴近学生的生活。

交际教学法

交际教学法

张冬倩

1. 交际教学法的定义

交际教学法(Communicative Approach, 简称交际法)也叫交际派语言教学法(Communicative Language Teaching Approach),是以培养交际能力为目的,以语言的功能项目为纲的一种教学方法体系,是设计教学大纲的一种途径。交际法也被称为功能法(Functional Approach)、意念法(Notional Approach)、功能—意念法(Function-Notional Approach)。功能是指语言行为,即用语言叙事和交流思想。意念是功能作用的对象,即特定交际需要和目标所表达的思想内容。例如,询问邮局的方位:Is there a post office near here? 询问是功能,"邮局"和"附近"是意念。功能和意念两个要素在运用语言叙述事情、表达思想的交际过程中是互相联系的。

2. 交际教学法的历史和发展

20 世纪后期可谓是知识爆炸的时代,科学技术的飞跃发展使人类社会进入知识经济时期,更大地促进了政治、经济、科技与文化的交流。对于传递信息的主要工具——语言,人们更重视其传递和负荷信息的作用。因此,外语教学领域必然从单纯的学习心理过程的研究转向语言应用的社会环境,即把语言的社会功能作为教学的主要内容,并更强调把社会需要作为外语学习的动力。交际法就是在这样历史背景中诞生的。成立于 1958 年的欧洲共同市场,1973 年由于英国、丹麦等国的加入而成为欧洲经济共同体(European Economic Community),各成员国之间的联系和合作更加密切。这些国家讲 9 种不同的语言,沟通之难,可想而知。为了迅速消除语言障碍,必须尽快掌握一门通用的外语——英语。因此交际法首先出现于西欧,并最早应用于英语教学,也就成为顺理成章的事。

交际法主要是在英国兴起的,其创始人是英国语言学家威尔金斯(D. A. Wilkins),主要代表人物有英国学者 J. L. Trim、荷兰学者 J. A. van Ek、L. G. Alexander 和 H. G. Widdowson 等。它的理论主要来自 20 世纪 60 年代兴起、70 年代形成高潮的社会语言学、人本主义心理学、20 世纪 60 年代后期兴起的心理语言学和乔姆斯基(Chomsky)的转换生成语法。尤其是社会语言学家海姆斯(Hymes)的交际能力理论和功能主义语言学家韩礼德(Halliday)的功能语言理论和话语分析理论以及威多森(Widdowson)的语言交际观。

"交际能力"这一概念是由社会语言学家海姆斯针对乔姆斯基的"语言能力"提出的。他认为,一个人的语言能力不仅包括乔姆斯基提出的能否造出合乎语法句子的语言能力,而且还包括能否恰当地使用语言的能力。由此他首次提出了包含“语言能力”和“语言运用”两个方面的交际能力。韩礼德的功能语言理论认为，语言的主要功能有以下七个。

(1)工具功能：用语言获取他物；

(2)调节功能：用语言控制他人的行为；

(3)互动功能：用语言与他人交往；

(4)人际功能：用语言表达个人感情和意义；

(5)启发功能：用语言学习和发现；

(6)想象功能：用语言创造一个想象的世界；

(7)表达功能：用语言交流信息。

交际学派认为，语言教学的目的是培养学生使用目的语进行交际的能力，语言教学的内容不仅要包括语言结构，还要包括表达各种意念和功能的常用语句。交际法重视培养学生的语言能力，采用真实、地道的语言材料，主张句型加情景来学习语言，鼓励学生多多接触和使用外语。运用交际法编写的最有名的教材是《跟我学》(*Follow Me*)。

交际法自从20世纪70年代问世以来，已有40多年的历史。培养学生的外语交际能力早已成为世界各国外语教学的目标。中华人民共和国成立后我国外语教学在方法论上的演变大致经历了如下几个时期：

(1)由1949年到20世纪60年代，基本上是原封不动地继承了传统的语法翻译法。

(2)20世纪60年代初引入了以行为主义心理学和结构主义语言学为理论依据的听说法，几年后，“文化大革命”爆发，外语教学一夜之间销声匿迹。

(3)20世纪80年代初，国家实行改革开放政策，外语教育吸取了以意念功能为主要理论基础的交际法的先进观念，结合我国国情，综合听说法在我国仅有的几年实践经验，大胆采用了结构功能大纲(Structional-notional Syllabus)并与国外语言学家合作，编写了相关的教材。此后经过20年的实践，伴随着市场经济的发展，对外语人才的迫切需求，交际法在我国已经初步扎下了根，并与时俱进，形成了有中国特色的交际教学法。

随着全球化进程的加快，各种多媒体的普及，课堂上师生之间交互活动的加强和学生在生活中越来越多的使用英语的机会，以培养交际能力为目的的交际教学法将会有更好、更快的发展。

3. 交际教学法的主要特点

交际法认为，语言是交际的工具，是为社会的全体成员服务的。由于人们的职业不同，对语言的要求和需要就不同，这就自然地影响到语言教学的内容、训练的形式、教学的方法和检查其效果的方法。如果根据生活实际，把交际中要表达的意念或思想、感情进行研究和归类，收集表达各种意念最常用的语句，并有计划地把这些语句教给学生，一定会收到事半功倍的效果。因此提出以意念为纲来组织语言材料，安排教学内容。同时，由于人们的社会地位和身份不同，说话的目的和场合有异，使用的语言也随之变化，因而教学对象应该是语言的交际功能。交际法的基本教学单位是话语(discourse)，它是传达信息的连续话语，或是具有语境的一段话，既立足于语言形式，又具有交际功能。

交际教学法的主要教学思想是内容决定形式，即根据学生学习外语的具体目的和交际要求来挑选相应的教学内容，采用相应的方法。教学原则是有目的性的：需要什么就学什么。交际法的语言观认为，语言是表达意义的系统，其基本功能是社会交际，语言学不应仅仅研究语言的形式，更要关注语言要完成的社会功能以及语言在人们社会交往中受到的制约因素。因此，第二语言教学的目的不仅是让学习者掌握语言规则、能正确地运用语言，更要掌握语言的使用规则，得体地运用语言。交际法强调以学生为中心，首先要分析学习者对第二语言的需要，教学内容和教学方法的确定都必须从学习者的需要出发。交际法还认为，学习者在言语中出现一些错误是正常的，也是不可避免的现象，学习者所追求的不可能是完美无缺的交际，而只能是有缺陷的但有效的交际，因此，对学习者的语言错误不应苛求。

4. 交际教学法在外语学校的具体运用

外语学校作为中学英语教学的最高层次，长期以来都坚持实施素质教育，选用先进的教材，采用国际流行的科学的英语教学法，强调课程从学生的学习兴趣、生活经验和认知水平出发，发展学生的综合语言运用能力，使语言学习的过程成为学生形成积极的情感态度、主动思维和大胆实践、提高跨文化意识和形成自主学习能力的过程。因此，强调语言功能的交际教学法也是外语学校常用的一种教学方法。

交际法的具体特点如下：

(1)以培养交际功能为宗旨，明确提出第二语言教学目标是培养创造性地运用语言的交际能力，不仅要求语言运用的正确性，还要求得体性。也就是说要知道在什么场合运用什么语言。

比如张冬倩老师在讲授 Food and Drink 这一课时，通过课件制作的动画，将学生带入到一个“餐厅”中，并遇到了一个“侍者”，后面的内容就是“侍者”和“顾客”(也就是学生)之间的对话，学生在回答侍者问题的同时，也是在学习新的句型，同时也知道了他们所学的句子所运用的场合是在餐厅，并且是在点菜的时候用的。

(2)以功能意念为纲。根据学习者的实际需要，选取真实自然的语言材料，而不是经过加工后的“教科书语言”。

比如彭华老师在教授 Movies 这一课的时候，在 Activate(激活)部分就使用了大量的和学生的现实生活非常贴近的影视图片，其中有当时热映的影片，有广为人知的影片，也有学生看过的很熟悉的影片，选择的材料和设计的活动都非常贴近生活，让学生身临其境地感受氛围。而后彭老师专门选择了七部极具代表性的电影，层层推进，告诉学生如何从不同的方面对影片进行评论，所选的材料真实自然，学生自然也接受得快，掌握得好。武汉实验外国语学校现阶段广泛使用的教材《展望未来》(*Look Ahead*)，每个单元都大量选取真实的生活文本，配套的视频材料频繁出现英美人士的真实访谈，均为学生提供了真实、自然的语言材料，而且相互联系，自成一体，非常适合交际教学法的需要。

(3)教学过程交际化。交际既是学习的目的，也是学习的手段，在教学中创造接近真实交际的情景并多采用小组活动的形式，通过大量言语交际活动培养运用语言交际的能力，并把课堂交际活动与课外生活中的交际结合起来。

比如张冬倩老师将学生分成小组，每个小组开一个不同的“餐厅”，大家互相去不同的“餐厅”，并用刚学的句型点菜。雷佼老师最后让学生以小组为单位设计一个访谈节目，采访名人和普通人，谈论他们不同的日常生活。彭华老师让学生两三人一组，模仿课文对话(鼓励学生做改动)，上台表演，完成整堂课的教学任务：评论一部电影。他们都是尽量创造真实的交际环境，通过大量言语交际活动培养学生运用语言交际的能力，并把课堂交际活动与课外生活中的交际结合起来。

(4)以话语为教学的基本单位。认为语言不是存在于孤立的词语或句子中，而是存在于连贯的语篇中。

比如全国外国语学校的统编教材《综合英语教程》中每个单元的第一部分 Getting Started 和第二部分 Chat Room 中的 Dialogue 的内容基本就是按照交际教学法的要求来编写的，其基本教学单位不是以单词而是以话语的形式出现的，内容重在培养学生的言语交际能力。而《看听学》的每个单课课文就是日常生活中的生动一幕，是一个生动的“情景”，而每个双课则是对前面单课中出现的基本句型进行总结和强化，该教材是交际法中典型的通过句型加情景来学习语言的一个范本。

外语学校的教师在教授英语时，很少单独解释单词的意思和用法，通常都是在句型练习中进行单词替换，比如：I would like to have…， I/ My father/ My mother always …让学生在连贯的语篇中学习语言。

(5)单项技能训练与综合性技能训练相结合，以综合性训练为主，最后达到在交际中综合运用语言的目的。

外语学校的英语课不像大学的专业课，重点是培养学生的基本语言能力，激发他们学习语言的兴趣，所以每节英语课可以说是听、说、读、写的综合操练，只是因教学目标的不同，侧重点有所不同而已，所以学校的课堂教学方式也会有听说课、精读课、复习课等的不同。

(6)对学习者在学习过程中出现的语言错误有一定的容忍度，不影响交际的错误能不纠正就不纠，尽量鼓励学习者发挥言语交际活动的主动性和积极性。即把流畅(fluency)放在比准确(accuracy)更为重要的位置上。

(7)交际法强调以学生为中心，强调教学要为学生的交际需要服务，以语言功能为纲。根据学以致用的原则，针对不同专业的学习者安排“专用语言”的教学。

(8)主张采用多种教学手段，不应仅仅是一本教科书，而应该是“教学包”，即教师用书、辅导读物、磁带、挂图、录像、电影、电视等辅助教学。

比如彭华、雷佼和张冬倩老师都使用了 PPT 制作的课件，其中都有大量信息丰富的图片，雷佼老师还插入了一段和教学内容相关的视频，让学生观看、思考并回答问题。多媒体教学以及 PPT 课件中多种多媒体材料(图片、音频、视频等)的使用在外语学校的外语教学中已十分常见。

(9)让学生处于情景之中，身临其境地感受氛围，用英语进行交际，是交际教学法的精髓。

比如雷佼老师在教授 Daily Routine 一课时，通过大量的和日常活动休戚相关的图片，将学生带到日常的生活和活动的场景中去谈论自己的活动以及父母的活动。彭华老师在教授 Movies 一课时，就通过大量影片的图片将学生带入到电影的世界中去。张冬倩老师通过课件制作的动画将学生带到某个餐厅，并遇到了一个“侍者”。她们都让学生身临其境地感受不同的场景，然后用所学的语言进行交际：雷佼老师是让学生学会谈论日常活动；彭华老师是让学生学会谈论电影；张冬倩老师则是让学生学会点菜。

5. 交际教学法的优点和不足

交际法博采众长，从当代语言学和心理学研究的最新成果中获取营养，受到诸如社会语言学、人类语言学、功能主义语言学、语用学、话语语言学、跨文化交际学、言语行为理论、语言变体研究直到中介语理论的影响。交际法是迄今为止影响最大、最富有生命力的外语教学法流派，对我国外语教学和对外汉语教学产生了很大的影响并已成为世界上影响最大的外语教学法流派之一，培养交际能力几乎成为世界各国外语教学最普遍的宗旨。

它的优点：

(1)重视学生的实际需要和交际能力的培养。摒弃了传统教学法那种只注重学生英语知识的掌握、语法分析、句子翻译，而轻视语言运用的能力，情景会话少，交际能力欠佳的缺点，要求不仅要培养学生听、说、读、写等方面的语言技能，还要教他们将这些语言技能灵活地运用到英语交际中去，有利于学生在一定的社会环境中恰当地使用目的语进行交际，体现了语言学习的最终目的。

(2)教学过程交际化和促进专用英语的发展。

它的缺点：

(1)功能项目问题：如何确定功能项目？确定语言功能项目的标准是什么？不同的第二语言教学需要多少语言功能范畴？如何科学地安排功能项目的教学顺序？等等，这些问题都没有很好地得到解决。

(2)没能处理好语法知识的教学问题：用意念功能范畴不能完全取代传统的语法知识，强调语法教学只学使用(use)、不学用法(usage)，这实际上是行不通的；而培养语法意识又会影响能力的培养等。然而现行的交际教学法在词汇教学上缺乏有效的办法及系统的分布，所以在整个中学阶段只能使学生掌握单词 2 000 个左右，而这样一个词汇量对于阅读中等难度的外文材料显然是不够的。

Teaching Plan of *An Integrated English Course* Book Ⅲ Unit 4 Item 1

教师：彭华

Teaching Aims:

1. Lead the students to comment on a film in simple English.
2. Introduce the prizes in Oscar and let the students comment on the films we've seen at school (from the acting, directing, music, etc.).
3. Make a similar dialogue.

Teaching Objects:

The students in Class Two, Junior Two.

Language Points:

1. Let the students express their opinions by using "I (don't) think that ...".
2. New words and expressions: romance, romantic, moving, classic, a big picture, fantastic, brilliant, a bit of, kind of
3. Important sentences: What do you think of it? I think/thought that ... I don't/didn't think that ...

Teaching Aids:

Multi-media teaching aid.

Teaching Methods:

Communicative Approach.

Teaching Procedures

Activate

在课堂教学开始前的较短时间内灵活安排新颖的导入活动，促使全班学生集中注意力，迅速进入学习状态。

Step 1

A student's duty show: introduce her favorite film to the whole class.

Step 2

1. Let the students guess which is the most expensive film in the world. Ask why so much money is needed and what is good in this film.

2. Ask them what films they have seen a lot, and then lead the question: What are important in a film?

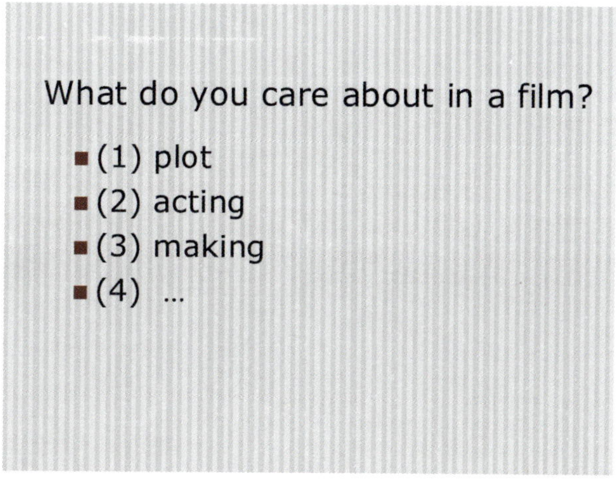

<table>
<tr>
<td>

Build

运用综合教学方法指导教学设计，营造良好的学习氛围，使学生快乐、自然、轻松、有效地学习语言。

</td>
<td>

1. When we ask a person's opinion of a film, we may say *What do/did you think of the film?* or *How do/did you like it?* Answer: *I think/thought that ...*
2. Give them pictures from some movies: *Garfield*, *Titanic*, *the Rock*, *The Lord of the Ring*, *In the Mood for Love*, *A Simple Noodle Story*. First let the students talk about them, then give some comments as examples. In those comments, there are some new words and expressions, just like *classic*, *moving*, *a bit of*, *kind of*, *etc.*
Garfield: fat, lazy, cute, funny, humorous.
Titanic: moving, classic, sad. The music is classic. (*adj.*) The song is classic, too. The film is a classic. (*n.*)
The Rock: adventure, exciting. The actors are really great. Their acting is amazing.
The Lord of the Ring: It has brilliant special effects.
In the Mood for Love: beautiful costume Chi-pao.
A Simple Noodle Story: boring, not funny at all.
Encourage the students to use *I think/ I don't think ...*
Tell them to put **NOT** in the main part of the sentence.
3. Give the students some examples of the comments on the films people like and dislike.

some comments on a film you like

- It's marvelous!
(great/terrific/wonderful/brilliant...)
- It's so romantic/moving... ! I cried!
- It's one of the greatest movies that I have ever seen. You can't miss it.
- He is just the one for the film.
- It's worth your time and money!

</td>
</tr>
</table>

some comments on a film you don't like

- I don't think it's good.
- It's a waste of time and money.
- It's a big NO NO. I just slept through.
- This is the worst film that I've ever seen.
- It's confusing! What is it talking about?
- It's rubbish! Bad acting, bad making, bad music! I can't bear it!

Cultivate

按照启发式教学原则，设计饶有趣味的训练来充分调动学生学习的主动性。

Go to Item 1 *The English Patient.* Simply introduce the film to the class.

The English Patient has won 9 Oscars.

The English Patient

- **Won**, Best Picture
- **Won**, Best Actress in a Supporting Role
- **Won**, Best Art Direction-Set Decoration
- **Won**, Best Cinematography
- **Won**, Best Costume Design
- **Won**, Best Director
- **Won**, Best Film Editing
- **Won**, Best Music
- **Won**, Best Sound

Explain the prizes one by one.

Turn to page 64. Finish the exercises.

Listen and repeat the sentences. Explain the language points in them.

Develop 设计真实的语言环境来综合概括构建及养成部分所传达的语言信息，巩固课堂教学、衔接新旧知识、贯通前后内容，帮助学生学习训练，复习巩固。	Show them some films they've seen at school, and ask their opinions of the films. Which is your favorite? Why do you like it so much? 
Evaluate 评估教学活动的实际效果，分析学习成效，帮助学生排除学习障碍。	1. Ask the students to make a similar dialogue with their partners in class. Give them comments immediately. 2. Ask the students to finish Exercise 3, 4, 5 in the workbook after class.

Notes:

1. The language points are in the book.
2. Pay attention to the position of ***not***.

课程设计及反思

教师：彭华

这堂课的教学内容选取的是《英语综合教程》初中二年级第一学期 Unit 4 的 Item 1，是一节精读课。

Item 1 是一篇对话，谈话的内容是关于美国大片《英国病人》的观影感受，属于简单的电影评论。让学生掌握相关的语言规则、学会初步的评论表达是这堂课的主要目的。整堂课大量使用了交际教学法。

整个课堂分为五大部分。在第一部分(Activate)中，我以当时的热映影片《阿凡达》引入，展示给学生什么是大片，为什么被称为大片，好在哪里……接下来问学生有没有很感兴趣并多次观看，甚至读过原版小说的电影，看了多少遍，等等。这是一个学生很感兴趣的话题，每个学生都有自己喜爱的电影、小说，可以做到有话可说，这很容易激发学生的自豪感：我看得多，我知道得多。其次，我介绍了一些自己比较感兴趣的电影，希望能赢得部分学生的共鸣，像电影《飘》、《哈利波特》、《傲慢与偏见》等。最后，讨论得出，对于一部电影人们通常比较关心的方面：情节、表演、制作、其他(音乐、服装等)。这是电影评论的第一步：从哪里入手。交际教学法要求教学者选择的材料和设计的活动都要尽量贴近生活，让学生处于情景之中，身临其境地感受氛围，他们才更能用英语进行交际。

交际教学法认为根据生活实际，把交际中要表达的意念、思想、感情进行研究和归类，收集表达各种意念最常用的语句，并有计划地把这些语句教给学生，一定会收到事半功倍的效果。所以在第二个部分(Build)中，我选择了七部极具代表性电影，《加菲猫》、《泰坦尼克》、《石破天惊》、《指环王》、《花样年华》、《死神来了》和《三枪》。每部影片的图片出来后我都会先问一下学生的观点，随后表明自己的观点。所给的句子中会出现后面课文中的新词，我及时给予了讲解。由于选取的每部影片都有很突出的方面，如情节生动感人、表演精彩、特效好……我的观点实际上也是一种启发，向学生示范：怎样去评论情节，评论表演等。在这个版块的最后，我做了个总结，哪些词语、句子可以用于受欢迎的影片，哪些可以用于不受欢迎的影片。同时我留有时间，让学生补充，还可以怎样去表达。

第三个部分(Cultivate)回到了课本，我先简单介绍了文中谈论的电影《英国病人》，给他们展示了电影的一个小片段，让学生对这个病人有个大致的认识，并简单介绍了故事情节。之后展示了它所获得的奥斯卡奖项，这个环节里会涉及奥斯卡文化介绍。随后是常规教学，采用了视听教学法的一些方法。听第一遍，主题理解；听第二遍，细节理解；第三遍，听读训练；最后，听(读)模仿。确信学生已能正确理解、朗诵所学句型。这个部分也是整堂课的重点之一。

语言学习的目的是为了使用语言。这就需要教学过程交际化，交际既是学习的目的，也是学习的手段，在教学中创造接近真实交际的情景并多采用小组活动的形式，通过大量言语交际活动培养运用语言交际的能力，并把课堂交际活动与课外生活中的交际结合起来。因此在第四部分(Develop)中，我将以前所有影视欣赏课上放过的电影截图放在一起，让学生选出自己的最爱，并讲明原因。评出最好的演员、情节、音乐等。在这个阶段，学生可以自由发言。事实上，学生的反应非常活跃，不断涌现出令人惊叹的句子，已远远超出我所给的例句。学生由于性格不同，喜好差别很大。如有的喜欢恐怖电影，有的喜欢浪漫爱情片，所选的最好影片、演员差别也很大。这就引起了争论与互动，不断有人补充，气氛活跃。个人回答之后，是小组表演，这也是最后一部分(Evaluation)，我让学生两三人一组，模仿课文做个对话(鼓励学生做改动)，上台表演，完成整堂课的教学任务：评论一部电影。对学生的表演以鼓励为主，并做简单的评论，之后布置作业，本课结束。

Teaching Plan of *An Integrated English Course* Book 1 Unit 9 Dialogue 2

教师：张冬倩

Teaching Aims:

1. To get the students to understand the dialogue.
2. To get the students to be familiar with some expressions in ordering and offering food and drink.
3. To get the students to master some new words.

Teaching Objects:

The students in Junior One.

Language Points:

1. Expressions in ordering and offering food and drink.
2. Vocabulary: restaurant, order, rare, medium, well done, and names for food and drink

Teaching Aids:

Multimedia, tap-recorder, blackboard and chalk.

Teaching Methods:

1. Audio-visual Method.
2. Communicative Approach.
3. Task-based Approach.

Teaching Procedures

Activate

在课堂教学开始前的较短时间内灵活安排新颖的导入活动，促使全班学生集中注意力，迅速进入学习状态。

Step 1　Greetings and Duty Report

1. T: Good afternoon, boys and girls. How are you today?
2. Student's Duty Show
3. Teacher's Comments

Step 2　Warm-up Activities

T: Do you have your lunch? Where do you often have your lunch?
(Teaching flash: The pictures of the school canteen.)

Teacher: Do you like to eat in the school canteen?

Step 3　Presentations

1. Lead in

T: Class, do you like eating? And I like eating, too. Where would you like to go for lunch most?

2. An Expressing Game

On the screen, the teacher shows the students pictures of different eating places, such as a café, a fast food restaurant, a cafeteria and a restaurant and asks the students to say where they would like to go for lunch by using "I'd like to go to..." Then the screen stops at the picture of a restaurant. A cartoon waiter greets them with: "Would you like to order, please?" (Teaching flash: a picture of a menu appears with the waiter's greetings, thus the students knows the meaning of "menu" and "order".)

a fast food restaurant

a restaurant

a waiter with greetings

B uild

运用综合教学方法指导教学设计，营造良好的学习氛围，使学生快乐、自然、轻松、有效地学习语言。

Go on with the expressing game with the teaching flash.

T= the teacher S= the student W= the waiter on the screen

T：Who is he?

S：A waiter.

T：What does he say?

Ss repeat：Would you like to order, please?

T：Class, are you ready to order? Now let's see the food.

(Teaching flash：different kinds of meat is shown on the screen, with a pattern "I'd like some ________.")

S：(Look at the pictures and say) I'd like some...

(Words：pork, mutton/ lamb, chicken, fish, beef, steak)

I'd like some pork.

	I'd like some mutton. I'd like some chicken. I'd like some fish.

I'd like some beef.

I'd like some steak.

(Teaching flash: at last, the computer stops at the steak.)

W: How would you like the steak? Rare, medium or well done?

(Teaching flash: pictures help the students understand the words "rare", "medium" and "well done".)

How would you like the steak?

Rare?

Medium?

	 S: (Look at the pictures and say) I'd like a ________ steak. (Words: rare, medium, well done)  W: Would you like a salad, too? W: What vegetables would you like?

(Teaching flash: different kinds of vegetables are shown on the screen with a pattern"I'd like to have some ________.")

S: (Look at the pictures and say) I'd like to have some...

(Words: cabbage, mushroom, eggplant, carrot, beans)

I'd like to have some cabbage.

I'd like to have some mushroom.

I'd like to have some eggplant.

I'd like to have some beans.

	W: Would you like anything to drink?  (Teaching flash: different kinds of drinks are shown on the screen with a pattern "I would like ______.") S: (Look at the pictures and say) I'd like ... (Expressions: a cup of tea, a packet of milk, a glass of lemonade, a bottle of juice, a glass of beer, a glass of wine, a tin of cola)  I would like a cup of tea.

I would like a packet of milk.

I would like a glass of lemonade.

I would like a bottle of juice.

I would like a glass of wine.

I would like a tin of Cola.

Thus the students are familiar with the basic expressions of "I'd like to go to...", "I'd like to have some...", "I'd like some/a..." in "Getting Started" and the words of food and drink.

T: So class, today we are going to study Unit 9 Food and Drink. (Teaching flash: the title of the unit.)

Unit 9 Food and Drink

Cultivate

按照启发式教学原则，设计饶有趣味的训练来充分调动学生学习的主动性。

Step 1　Oral Procedure

1. Listening and Understanding (Books shut)

   Questions for understanding:

   (1) Where are they? (They are in a restaurant.)

   (2) Does the man want a beef? (No, he doesn't.)

   (3) How does he like it? (He wants a rare one.)

   (4) What salad does he like? (He wants some fresh green beans.)

   (5) What does the man drink? (He wants a glass of Sprite.)

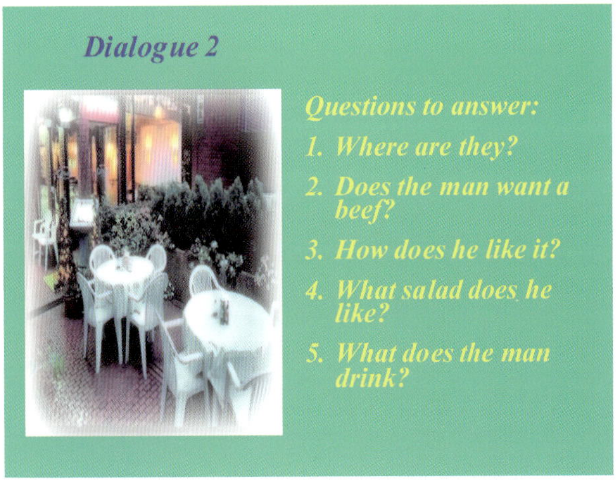

2. Listening (Books open)
3. Listening and Chorus Repetition (Books open)
4. Listening and Individual Repetition (Books open)
5. Reading Aloud

Waiter: Would you like to order, please?
Diner: Yes, I'd like a steak and chips, please.
W: How would you like the steak?
Rare, medium or well done?
D: Rare.
W: Would you like a salad,too?
D: Yes, please.
W: What vegetables would you like?
We've got fresh green beans.
D: OK. I'd like to have some.
W: Would you like anything to drink?
D: Yes. A glass of Sprite, please.
W: Yes, sir.

Step 2　Scene Acting

Ask the students to act this dialogue.

Develop

设计真实的语言环境来综合概括构建及养成部分所传达的语言信息，巩固课堂教学、衔接新旧知识、贯通前后内容，帮助学生学习训练，复习巩固。

Activity

1. The teacher shows different kinds of food on the screen and lets the students discuss and tell the order of the food to have in a western restaurant.

   Keys：soup→main course→salad→dessert→drink

2. Divide the students into four groups and ask the students to open a restaurant of their own; they can make a menu and be the waiter. The students from other groups may be the diner and try to order their favourite food; they can do this in front of the class. An example menu is given to them on the screen.

MAYFLOWER RESTAURANT

MENU

STARTERS

Soup………………..$2.95

……………………………

MAIN COURSES

Steak………………..$13.00

……………………………

DESSERT

Salad………………..$3.25

……………………………

DRINKS

Water………………..$1.50

……………………………

GroupWork:

Please have a restaurant of YOURS :

You can use these sentences:

For waiter: Can I help you?

What would you like to eat/drink?

Would you like something to eat/drink?

For diner: I'd like a/some…

I'd like to have a/some…

Evaluate

评估教学活动的实际效果，分析学习成效，帮助学生排除学习障碍。

Step 1　Conclusions

The teacher lets the students come to the front and tell the others what he orders in the restaurant.

A Song：Pease Pudding

Step 2　Assignment

Recite Dialogue 1 and make new dialogues with the partner.

Notes:

Attachment: The Text

W: Would you like to order, please?

D: Yes, I'd like a steak and chips, please.

W: How would you like the steak? Rare, medium or well done?

D: Rare.

W: Would you like a salad, too?

D: Yes, please.

W: What vegetables would you like? We've got fresh green beans.

D: OK. I'd like to have some.

W: Would you like anything to drink?

D: Yes. A glass of Sprite, please.

W: Yes, sir.

课程设计及反思

教师：张冬倩

我的这节课选取了《综合英语教程》第一册第九单元 Getting Started 和 Dialogue 2 的有关食物和饮料的重点句型、食物和饮料的名称以及对话部分，是一节听说课。

我这节课的主要教学目的是让学生了解食物与饮料的名称以及如何在餐馆中点菜。其中在词汇方面要求学生学会说食物与饮料的名称，句型方面要能学会在餐馆中点菜以及侍者的服务用语，聊天室的场景设在一个快餐厅和一个西餐厅。其难点在于食物和饮料的名称很多，难以记忆。但也有优势，那就是学生对食物和饮料这一话题一向就比较感兴趣，如果掌握得当，可以使其对单词的记忆变得相对简单。在授课过程中我使用了交际教学法和任务型教学法。

该课程的具体步骤如下所示(伴随多媒体制作的动画课件的辅助)：

激活(Activate)：教师通过与学生的简短聊天，知道他们对“吃”很感兴趣，接下来播放课件，屏幕上依次出现快餐厅和西餐厅，并由此问学生：“Where would you like to go? A fast food restaurant or a restaurant?”并让学生使用“I would like to go to...”这一句型来表达他们的喜好。

构建(Build)：接下来教师带学生们走进一家西餐厅，遇到一个侍者(课件中的)，他会问：“Would you like to order, please?”学生当然想点菜了，但首先是主菜，屏幕上出现的是各种肉类和鱼肉，学生可以看着出现的肉食，选择他们想要的。此时教师可引导他们说：“I'd like some...”如此就解决了有关肉食的词汇问题。接下来侍者又会问：“How would you like the steak? Rare, medium, or well done?”屏幕上会出现这三个词的相关图解，学生通过图解可了解关于牛排生熟的提问，教师引导他们说：“I'd like a ... steak.”以此将三个生词教给学生，图解可以使这三个新词很快被学生理解、接受，并学会用这些词来表达自己的喜好。接下来还要点 salad 和 drink，屏幕上的侍者总会在学生们选了他们想要的某样食物后提出下一个食物的选项，这样在教师的指导下，食物与饮料的名称、点菜的句型已被学生接受了不少。点菜的任务也完成了。接下来是对课文的理解，有了前面的铺垫，学生可以很容易地理解对话发生的场合及主人公的喜好。

在以上两个步骤中，首先在激活(Activate)阶段，教师向学生展现每课要学习的主要语言结构。教师通过交际教学法，从基本的语言结构入手，有意设置了一个情景——餐厅，通过情景性的语言操练，让学生在情景之中身临其境地感受氛围，从而学会并掌握在实际交际活动中使用语言的本领。这个从语言结构到交际本领的学习过程是学生由语言方面的能力向实际运用语言的能力转化的过程，因为培养交际能力是语言教学的最终目的。

在第三步构建(Build)中，教师让学生通过快速反应、句型转换和操练，掌握本节课最基本的语言结构：I would like.../ I would like to... 主要通过机械操练，为下一阶段的情景操练做准备。而学生也通过多媒体设置的情景性的语言操练，学习了有关的食物和饮料的单词，并掌握了在实际交际活动中使用英语点菜的本领。

养成(Cultivate)：学习完对话后，可以要求学生进行表演，看他们是否真的理解了。

发展(Develop)：活动一：课件中出现各种不同的食物，比如说 ice-cream，steak，coffee，vegetable 等，学生通过看动画图片排列点餐时的顺序，用以拓展他们对于英美饮食文化的了解。

活动二：接下来教师可以让学生们自己开餐馆，设菜单，让其他的同学来点菜，在完成任务的过程中活用所学句型与词汇。

这个步骤中，教师在教学中创造接近真实交际的情景并采用小组活动的形式，通过大量言语交际活动培养学生运用语言进行交际的能力，并把课堂交际活动与课外生活中的交际结合起来。

评价(Evaluate)：教师让学生到全班同学前面介绍自己在餐厅已点的东西，对各个小组的活动进行讲评。

本课的内容不多，但是涉及 would like something 和 would like to do 的句式结构，而且生词 rare，medium 和 well done 也不方便用英语解释，但通过利用课件做的图片，学生既可以了解生词，而且也会很愿意完成他们的交际任务。

整节课的课堂活动都以学生为中心，学生处于更为积极主动的地位。教师的作用既不是讲授语言知识，也不是指挥句型训练，而是通过各种途径组织学生进行交际活动，教师只是课堂交际活动的组织者或管理人。学生则是课堂活动的主体。教学活动有些由单个学生完成，有些则是通过小组合作。教学内容也是以学生的交际需要为依据的，学生学了就用，从而摆脱了被动接受知识的地位。

利用多媒体设置情景进行交际型教学，对教材没有特别的要求，只要课文的内容适应创设情景，就都可以利用。以上文的课件为例，任何其他的中学英语教材，只要涉及购物、就餐、看病、参观等社会活动的，基本上都可以套用上面的模式，所以利用多媒体设置情景进行交际型教学，在中学英语中是可行而且也可以被广泛使用的，培养学生的外语交际能力早已成为世界各国外语教学的目标。

Teaching Plan of *Integrated English Course* Book I Unit 3 Getting Started Exercise 4 & Dialogue 1

教师：雷佼

Teaching Aims:

1. To let the students know how to express activities in their daily life.
2. To improve the students' comprehensive using of English.
3. To let the students enjoy speaking English.

Teaching Objects:

The students in Class One, Junior One.

Language Points:

1. present tense.
2. the using of the third person singular form.

Teaching Aids:

Multi-media teaching aid.

Teaching Methods:

1. Communicative Approach.
2. Audio-visual Method.
3. Task-based Approach.

Teaching Procedures

Activate

在课堂教学开始前的较短时间内灵活安排新颖的导入活动，促使全班学生集中注意力，迅速进入学习状态。

1. Greetings and duty report.
   After the duty report, the students are asked to give some comments on it.
2. Free talk about the students' life at weekends.

(1) What do you usually do at weekends?

(2) What does your father/mother often do at weekends?

(3) Show the students some pictures about activities at weekends and introduce new phrases such as *play chess*, *play the piano*, *ride a horse*, *work in the garden*, etc.

*B*uild

运用综合教学方法指导教学设计，营造良好的学习氛围，使学生快乐、自然、轻松、有效地学习语言。

1. Practice the mini-dialogue in Getting Started Exercise 4.

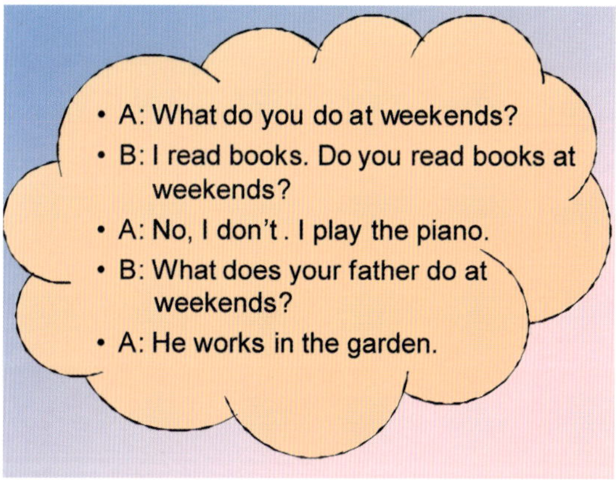

2. Pair work: Ask the students to make a similar dialogue by using the new phrases.
3. Talk about the students' daily routine on weekdays.

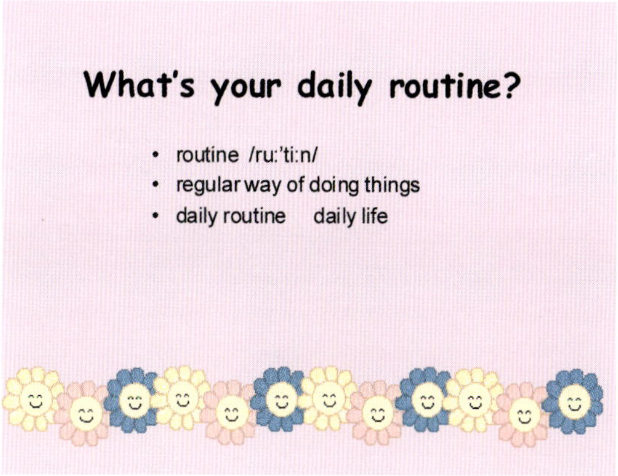

(1) Talk about their daily life at school

(2) Practice Dialogue One: John's Daily Routine

John's Daily Routine

- Linda: When do you get up every morning?
- John: I usually get up at six.
- Linda: Do you go to school at seven?
- John: Yes, I do. I am always early.
- Linda: What time does school begin?
- John: It begins at eight.
- Linda: When do you have lunch?
- John: At eleven thirty.
- Linda: When do you go home?

John: We usually have sports after school and go home at about five.

(3) Ask the students to change the dialogue into a monologue named "John's Daily Routine" according to the information in the following picture. The third person singular form is used.

***C*ultivate** 按照启发式教学原则，设计饶有趣味的训练来充分调动学生学习的主动性。	1. Watch a video about Kay Family's daily routine. Let the students answer some questions about their daily life. (1)When does the father get up every morning? (2)When does the family have breakfast? (3)What time does the daughter go to school? (4)What do they do at 7：30 every evening? **The Kay Family's Daily Routine**  2. Watch the video again and ask the students to take down notes about the Kay Family's daily routine. Then ask the students to retell it.
***D*evelop** 设计真实的语言环境来综合概括构建及养成部分所传达的语言信息，巩固课堂教学、衔接新旧知识、贯通前后内容，帮助学生学习训练，复习巩固。	**Group Work** Some group members play the role of VIPs like the US President Obama or pop star Jay Chou. The others play the role of ordinary people—people that the students are familiar with, such as their head teacher or foreign teacher. They sit together in a Talk Show. One of the group members plays as the host and interview them about their daily life. 

Evaluate 评估教学活动的实际效果，分析学习成效，帮助学生排除学习障碍。	**Evaluation Activity** Review what we have learned and practiced during this class. Task A　Write about Kay Family's daily life. Task B　Write about a famous person's daily life that you imagine and comment on it. (Do you like this way of life? Why or why not?) This assignment is asked to do by groups and the students can choose Task A or Task B.

Notes:

The Kay Family's Daily Routine 材料来源：《展望未来》第一册第 8 单元。

课程设计及反思

教师：雷　佼

我的这节课选取了《综合英语教程》第一册第三单元 Getting Started 中的 Exercise 4 和 Dialogue 1 两个部分，是一节听说课。这节课的教学目的在语法方面是让学生熟练掌握一般现在时态，尤其是一般现在时的单数第三人称形式。交际方面是让学生学会运用一般现在时表达日常生活的话题。这条主线十分清晰，所有活动都围绕这个教学目的展开。

我使用了交际教学法、任务型教学法和视听教学法。交际教学法贯穿于整堂课始终。从第一步 Activate（激活）教师与学生自由对话谈论周末活动到第二步 Build（构建）学生两人一组对话，互相谈论日常活动及最后拓展环节的小组活动，以访谈的形式谈论名人或熟悉的人的日常生活，都体现了交际教学法的核心观点，即培养学生用外语来进行交流的基本技能。通过这些交际活动，基础好的学生熟练掌握了一般现在时的用法并能自由运用这种时态谈论日常生活中的话题。基础一般的学生掌握了一般现在时的用法，能运用这种时态谈论日常生活的话题，但不够熟练。基础较弱的学生能听懂和配合谈论日常生活中的话题。在第三步 Cultivate（养成）环节，我运用了任务型教学法和视听教学法。看视频回答问题和用自己的语言复述视频内容这两项任务直观而有吸引力，基础好的学生能完成两个任务，基础弱的学生能完成第一个任务。第四步 Develop（拓展）环节让学生以小组为单位设计一个访谈节目，采访名人和普通人，谈论他们不同的日常生活，运用了任务型教学法。基础好的学生担任主持人或是主要发言人，能熟练用英语表达。基础弱的学生能担任配角参与到节目中。不过由于初一学生的英语表达能力有限，访谈内容不够丰富。

这节课主题明确，重点突出，层层推进，步步深入。完成和实现了教学目标，各个层次的学生都有收获。课堂中学生是主角，教师起引领者的作用，符合新课程标准的要求。从教学法的使用来看，任务型教学法和视听教学法运用得当，效果不错。在交际法的运用中，交际语境的真实性方面还有欠缺，为了让学生掌握和运用新词汇而忽视了交际本身的意义。例如，在中国很少有人周末“在花园劳作”。为了让学生练习“work in the garden”这个词组，我在让学生谈论周末的活动时给出了这个词组，这其实是与交际法的原则相悖的。更好的做法是加入一点文化背景上的介绍，介绍这是西方人过周末的一种典型方式。甚至可以在自由谈论时比较一下中西方周末活动的差异，这会使这节课更增色。

游戏教学法

游戏教学法

教师：蔡文静

一、游戏教学法的定义

游戏教学就是在教学中尽可能将枯燥的语言现象转变为学生乐于接受的、生动有趣的游戏形式，为学生创造丰富的语言交际情景，使学生在玩中学，学中玩。我们所提倡的互动语言教学认为小组活动有利于学生用目的语进行交际，而游戏就属于这种小组活动之一。游戏教学法是情景教学法的一种形式，是以一定的科学理论为基础的，旨在巩固课文教学、熟悉新单词、锻炼学生的语言实践能力、开发学生潜力与智力；是以实际教学内容为依据，按照一定的程序步骤和规则，循序渐进的英语活动。这种英语学习方式可以分为三个环节：游戏的准备阶段、课上的游戏进行阶段、评分或讨论阶段。“英语游戏教学法”是“游戏”和“英语教学”二者巧妙的结合体，并具有深厚的科学理论和课堂教学的实用价值。

二、历史与背景

把游戏运用到教学中的做法自古就有。从古希腊起，西方教育就不乏游戏与教学的论述以及把游戏用于教学中的实践。我国儿童教育家胡叔异 70 多年前在他的《小学游戏教学法》中就指出：“儿童喜欢做的事情，莫过于游戏。”

我国自古在游戏教学方面就有很多论述。程颐曾说：“教人未见意趣，必不乐学。”王守仁主张：“教童子，必使其趋向鼓舞，中心喜悦。”现代教育家吴冠杰曾说：“游戏能否搬到外语课堂上作为一种重要的组织形式？回答是肯定的。游戏作为一种学习形式远远早于课堂教学。学习语言通过游戏手段要比学校教育学习语言的历史早得多。通过游戏学英语，使学生在娱乐中学会语言，掌握语言，从而开发智力，发展智力，在游戏中找到学习英语的兴趣，真可谓寓教于乐。”

心理学家罗杰斯认为：人的认知活动总是伴随着一定的情感因素，当情感因素受到压抑甚至抹杀时，人的自我创造潜能就得不到发展和实现。而只有用真实的、对个人的尊重和理解学生内心世界的态度，才能激发学生的热情，增强他们的自信心。当课堂教学能引起学生学习的兴趣时，就可以充分调动学生的智力因素和非智力因素，使学生在学习中注意力集中的时间更为持久，更好地感知、记忆、思维和想象，从而更牢固、更多地掌握知识，获得技能。

《全日制义务教育普通高级中学英语课程标准》强调，教师应是学生学习的组织者、引导者和参与者。教学过程应是师生平等、共同发展互动的过程。教学应致力于创造一种无拘无束的轻松心理氛围，解除学生的思想顾虑。因此，英语游戏教学法的运用对于提高中小学英语课堂效果是非常有效的。

对比发达国家学校的课堂，我们的英语课堂存在一个明显的缺陷，就是刻板、枯燥、因循守旧、循规蹈矩，尽管这些年来不断地改进，但还是非常不够。兴趣是最好的老师，只有感兴趣了，才能充分调动主观能动性，才能最大限度地挖掘人的潜力。我们正是基于学生们必须要学习规定的知识和技能又承认和尊重他们的天性这两个方面，将二者巧妙合理地结合起来，创造了游戏教学法。

游戏教学法可以直接影响学生对学习英语的兴趣，有利于学生形成正确的学习方法和良好的学习习惯，有利于化难为易，有利于减轻学生的学习负担，符合素质教育的要求。

三、在外语学校的应用

英语教学当中有很多种游戏，按设计目的区分，教学游戏可分为操练性游戏、激趣性游戏、合作性游戏三大类。

1. 操练性游戏

(1)快速操练性游戏：这类游戏一般用在课前，为的是让学生快速地回忆单词、复习旧知。

例如在我校许妍琼老师这节课的 Activate(激活)环节里(详见下文的课例展示，后同)，她采用的是猜词游戏。在首字母的提示下，给学生想象的空间，再给出一定的提示，让学生们有限制地去猜。学生表现极其踊跃，争先恐后讲出自己想到的词。起到了调动课堂气氛的作用。同时，学生的思维也被打开，训练了学生对于词汇的联想能力。

又如在我校戴文曦老师的这节课里，首先以一个 Brainstorm 的接龙游戏，让学生说出一个和英国相关的名称，可以是名人，也可以是地名，不能及时说出的组被淘汰出局，坚持到最后的组为胜利者。这个游戏起点比较低，能够吸引学生积极参与，照顾到各个层次的学生，从 London 到 Harry Porter 等，由于要求说过的东西不能重复，花几分钟的时间可以让学生对英国文化、地理进行了解和复习。这里运用的就是游戏教学法。在课堂刚开始的时候用这样的活动进行热身，可以很好地吸引学生的注意力。

(2)反复操练性游戏：这类游戏一般用于新学完一组单词后，通过反复操练来巩固新知。

2. 激趣性游戏

这类游戏一般是为引出新知而设的，目的是激发学生继续学习的兴趣、启迪思维。

例如在我校张金霞老师这节课的 Activate(激活)环节中为了充分发挥学生自身的认知能力，调动他们已有的目的语资源，教师设计了一个竞猜游戏：先让学生们争相说出自己知道的职业名词，然后运用图片展示给学生更多的职业名词，让学生们以小组为单位进行“Who has a good memory?”游戏。学生们在轻松的气氛中快速记住了这些单词，并顺利过渡到下一环节。这样正好利用了学生的好奇心，激发他们动脑思考，继续学习。

3. 合作性游戏

这类游戏是以小组合作交流为主体开展的，可以是展示性的，也可以是竞赛性的。

(1)展示性合作游戏：以展示学习成果为目的。主要以角色表演和作品展示的方式来开展。

例如在我校向丹老师这节课的 Develop(发展)环节中，运用角色扮演的教学法使学生的语言技能得到拓展。制造生活情景，将学生分组，邀请学生扮演家庭角色并对校园生活进行评论，使用关键句型 too...to，so...that...，...enough...to。要求学生分组后自如运用所学的新句型完成任务，学生的综合语言运用能力在此环节中得到充分展示。

(2)竞赛性合作游戏：竞赛是学习、练习的一种好形式。

这一类游戏的代表是"我来描述你来猜"。教师将学生分组，引导学生用英语或动作表情来描述一件事物，请学生代表来猜。以猜得最准确、最快或是最多作为标准来选出获胜的小组。学生好胜心强，利用竞赛可以激发学生的兴趣，操练和巩固所学知识。竞赛一般可贯穿教学的全过程，也可在课程结束前进行决赛，分出胜负，培养学生的竞争意识。

例如在我校向丹老师这节课的 Activate(激活)环节，教师首先采用三张图片直观形象地说明 a little、very、too 的差异。然后进行价格猜测游戏：教师提供不同事物的照片，让学生分组猜测该物品的价格并不加思考地说出他们心中的估价，每组派一位代表上台，组员提示，提示语必须包含 too，little，very 这些较模糊的概念而非具体数字。差距最小的组获胜。汽车模型、房屋模型等的价格难以准确衡量，既会加深学生对这些表程度的形容词/副词的了解，又可以强化导入阶段的教学成果，并最大限度地调动学生的学习热情和参与课堂的积极性。

游戏能调动学生的学习热情，充分发挥学生学习的自觉性，那么游戏教学中如何合理有效地设计游戏，使游戏真正起到提高课堂效果的作用呢？在外语学校的英语课堂上，教师们始终遵循着以下几点英语课堂游戏设计的原则：

1. 游戏的设计要有趣味性

教育心理学表明，当教学能引起学生的兴趣时，就可使学生在学习中集中注意力，更好地感知、记忆、思维和想象，从而获得较多的、较牢固的知识和技能，并表现出喜悦和求知欲望。采用游戏教学的目的在于借助游戏的趣味性，使学生积极地参与到学习语言知识、掌握语言技能的各项活动中去。游戏的组织形式应不断激发学生的好奇心，尽量创设真实、有趣的语言情境，让学生主动、快乐、兴趣盎然地参与游戏。

2. 游戏的设计要有目的性

游戏是学生喜闻乐见的一种活动形式，但在设计时绝不能为玩而玩，盲目地迎合学生做游戏的心理，而忽略了游戏应该是课程的组成部分，是为教学目的服务的，是教师精心设计的产物。设计游戏应围绕教学目的进行，无论是复习旧知，还是操练新知，都不能淡化教学任务，破坏学生知识系统的形成，或毫无目的地进行，为了游戏而游戏。

3. 游戏的设计要有竞争性

中小学生的好奇心、好胜心强，教师在课堂上设计游戏要抓住学生争强好胜、集体荣誉感强的特点，要富有竞争性，使学生在游戏中掌握知识的过程变得生动，形成你追我赶积极向上的气氛。

4. 游戏的设计要有层次性

游戏的设计要面向全体学生。面向全体学生的核心思想是使每一个学生得到发展，因此在游戏活动中，就是要给每一位学生创造机会。教师要根据学生实际分层次开展游戏，这样，全体学生都能体验到成功的喜悦，个个都处于主动学习状态。

5. 游戏的设计要有灵活性

游戏要有灵活性是指在教学中要适时、适度开展游戏活动，形式要灵活多样，以免学生厌烦。游戏教学包罗万象，小至字母、单词，长至句子、短文、课本剧；组织形式有个人、两人、多人、集体等。在游戏中教师要注意课堂气氛与课堂节奏的调整与把握，灵活处理教材内容与游戏之间的关系，适当调整教学模式中的各个环节。

6. 游戏的设计要有规则性

每一项游戏活动都有其规律。在教学中进行的游戏活动必须是有序的，教师必须组织得当，游戏完成时才能达到目的，否则内容再好也失去了它的功效。因此教学游戏必须要受规则制约，要有内容呈现规则、时间限制规则、角色表演规则、竞赛规则等。要求学生遵守一定的纪律，既要放得开又要收得拢，养成有令即行、有禁即止的良好课堂习惯。

四、游戏教学法的优点与不足

游戏教学法的优点：

1. 激发学生学习英语的兴趣

孔子曰：“知之者不如好之者，好之者不如乐之者。”英国有一句名谚语：“Education must be fun.” 说明兴趣是学好语言的关键，激发学生学习英语的兴趣是中小学阶段英语教学的一项重要任务。在英语教学中恰当地运用游戏能够调节课堂气氛，引导学生积极参与课堂教学活动，有利于培养学生的兴趣，使课堂变得生动、有趣，符合“乐学”的原则。

2. 改变师生课堂角色，减轻师生的负担

在传统的教学中，教师是主体，学生是客体，书本是媒介。一节课采用的都是“教师讲，学生听；教师问，学生答；教师领，学生读”的模式，教师感觉疲惫，学生感觉乏味。

而在游戏活动中，教师是指导者、参与者，学生则是活动的主体。教师根据教学目标及教学内容设计的游戏指导起来轻松，学生学起来愉悦。在教学中强调学生的主体性，要求学生共同参与，体现了教师主导、学生主体作用的发挥。游戏教学中，充分利用学生的有意注意和无意注意，激发学生的学习动机，使学生积极参与课堂的教学活动，有利于化难为易，从而减轻师生的负担。

3. 有利于学生的身心发展

游戏教学符合中小学生的心理特点。它可以缓和课堂的紧张气氛，营造轻松的氛围。游戏通常具有比赛的性质，参加游戏的人都积极参与思维，有利于克服腼腆羞怯的心理障碍，提高并保持良好的身心愉悦的状态。合理的游戏规则，适当的奖惩，可以培养学生的组织性与纪律性。这些都有利于学生的心理健康发展。

游戏教学都包含智力成分，因此，游戏教学有利于开发学生的智力、记忆力、思维能力、观察力、想象力、创造力、判断力等，这些能力都在游戏中得到锻炼及提高。

游戏教学法的不足：

1. 喧宾夺主——游戏只为课堂气氛服务

随着游戏教学对英语课堂教学效果所产生的重要性不断增强，越来越多的年轻教师在英语课堂上使用游戏教学法。但不可否认的是，很多教师更注重游戏对课堂气氛所起的作用，从而忽视了游戏教学法的最本质的目的——通过游戏让学生提高兴趣，学到知识。

2. 只放不收——游戏成为课堂教学的绊脚石

由于很多教师对课堂和学生的掌控力有限，经常会有游戏活动一发不可收拾的情况出现。例如游戏结束了，课堂纪律无法维持，或是学生纠结于游戏中的某个细节，使得下一步的教学计划无法完成。所以一个游戏是否能成功地辅助课堂教学，还要求教师要勤修内功，进一步提高自己的专业能力。

Teaching Plan of *Integrated English Course* Book 3 Unit 2 Item 1

教师：戴文曦

Teaching Aims:

1. To get the students to learn about Eton College.
2. To get the students to learn to briefly introduce their school.

Teaching Objects:

Class 4.

Language Points:

found, go on with, be educated, provide sth. for sb., harsh, including, in the American sense, resident, overseas

Teaching Aids:

Multimedia and radio.

Teaching Methods:

1. Game Teaching Method.
2. Task-based Teaching Method.

Teaching Procedures

Activate 在课堂教学开始前的较短时间内灵活安排新颖的导入活动，促使全班学生集中注意力，迅速进入学习状态。	**Step 1 Greetings** **Step 2 Brainstorm: What do you know about Britain?** The students are divided into 4 groups. They are going to tell the teacher anything about Britain. It can be a name, a place, some famous people, a film, etc. They are going to speak out the thing in turn. The students who can't speak out immediately will lose. The group who can tell the most things will win the game.

Build

运用综合教学方法指导教学设计，营造良好的学习氛围，使学生快乐、自然、轻松、有效地学习语言。

Step 3　Lead in

Show the students some pictures about British Prime Ministers. They were former British Prime Ministers.

Cameron was educated in Eton. He went on with his study in Oxford.

Henry VI founded Eton College to provide free education for 70 poor scholars.

The school dress has always been a black tailcoat and waistcoat and pin-striped trousers.

Many famous people studied in Eton, including Prince William and Harry.

The school dress has always been a black tailcoat and waistcoat and pin-striped trousers. Many famous people studied in Eton, including Prince William and Harry.

Life in the early days was harsh.

extremely cruel, severe

Life in the early days was harsh.

It is now a secondary school,

a high school, in the American sense.

It is now a secondary school, a high school, in the American sense.

Cultivate

按照启发式教学原则，设计饶有趣味的训练来充分调动学生学习的主动性。

Step 4　Item 1

1. Listen and fill in the numbers in Ex. 1.
2. Listen and tell whether the following statements are true or false.

1. Listen and fill in the numbers in Ex. 1.

2. Listen and tell whether the following statements are True or False.

Eton College was founded by Willam VI. F

The school dress has always been a black tailcoat and waistcoat. T

Many famous people were educated in Eton College. T

The students in Eton are between the ages of 13 and 15. F

3. Listen and answer the questions.

Listening Questions

1. For whom was Eton College founded?

It was founded to provide free education for 70 poor scholars.

2. How was the life in the early days?

Harsh, rats ran free, boys washed outside, using only cold water.

3. What kind of school is it today?

Asecondary school, a high school to the American people.

4. Are all the students from Britain?

Most of them are residents in Britain. Some are from overseas.

4. Listen and read after the tape.

In 1440, Henry VI founded Eton College to provide free education for 70 poor scholars. They would then go on with their study at King's College, Cambridge.

Life in the early days was harsh. Rats ran free and the boys had to wash outside, using only cold water.

Eighteen former British Prime Ministers were educated in Eton, including the Duke of Wellington. The school dress has always been a black tailcoat and waistcoat and pin-striped trousers since the 1850s.

Today, Eton is a secondary school, a high school in the American sense, for about 1,280 boys between the ages of 13 and 18. Most of the boys are residents in the United Kingdom, but some are from overseas.

<table>
<tr>
<td>

*D*evelop

设计真实的语言环境来综合概括构建及养成部分所传达的语言信息，巩固课堂教学、衔接新旧知识、贯通前后内容，帮助学生学习训练，复习巩固。

</td>
<td>

Step 5　Development

Eton College is very famous and many famous people graduate from it. How about your school? Suppose 20 years later, you have become very successful in your field. In an interview, you talk about your secondary school life and introduce your school to the public.

</td>
</tr>
<tr>
<td>

*E*valuate

评估教学活动的实际效果，分析学习成效，帮助学生排除学习障碍。

</td>
<td>

Step 6　Homework

1. Recite Item 1.
2. Workbook Ex. 2 and 3.

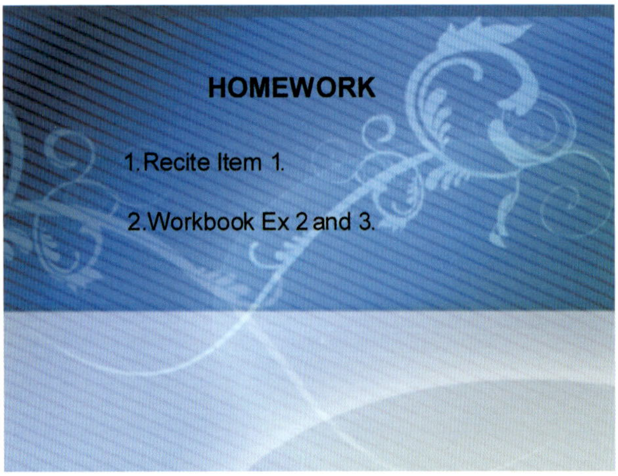

</td>
</tr>
</table>

课程设计及反思

教师：戴文曦

一、教学内容和目的

本课选取了《综合英语教程》第3册第2单元 Historic Places Item 1 部分，主要介绍英国著名学府伊顿公学，通过对这个 Item 的学习，使学生掌握一些相关的词汇、句型用以介绍自己的学校，并在最后 DEVELOP 环节中给每组学生一个成功人士的身份，在一次采访的活动中评价自己的学校。这是一节英语听说课。

二、教学过程

本课主要采用多媒体教学，运用了任务型教学法及游戏教学法。首先以一个 Brainstorm 的接龙游戏，让学生说出一个和英国相关的名称，可以是名人，也可以是地名，不能及时说出的组被淘汰出局，坚持到最后的组为胜利者。这个游戏起点比较低，能够吸引学生积极参与，照顾到各个层次的学生，从 London 到 Harry Porter 等，由于说过的东西不能重复，花几分钟的时间可以让学生对英国文化、地理进行了解和复习。这里运用的是游戏教学法。在课堂刚开始的时候用这样的活动进行热身，可以吸引学生的注意力。接下来通过对英国首相的介绍引入本课的主题——伊顿公学。介绍伊顿的历史、校服以及很多名人都在伊顿受过教育，将 Item 中的重点词汇引入，通过听文章填数字、判断正误以及回答问题来检验学生对文章的理解程度，这里运用的是任务型教学法，学生积极思考，能够发挥学生的主体性作用，易于保持学习的积极性，养成良好的学习习惯。最后在 DEVELOP 环节中，给每个小组一个成功人士的身份(外交部翻译官、著名演员、律师、著名企业的 CEO)，在小组内编一个访谈节目，谈论自己的母校。这里运用的也是游戏教学法。用 role-play 的方式，激发学生大胆地表达自己的想法，将课文的句式运用在自己的对话中，介绍自己的学校以及“早期”的学生生活，学生充分发挥自己的想象力，并和小组成员一起编出一段访谈的对话，既培养了学生的群体意识和合作精神，又培养了学生综合运用英语的能力。

三、教学反思

运用课堂游戏帮助教学改变了教师“一言堂”的教学模式，使得师生间、学生间可以平等交流。教师通过分组，使知识、能力、性格等方面各有差异的学生集合在一起，去发现别人的闪光点来启迪自己的思维。在游戏中，知识、能力、性格相互碰撞并升华。在游戏中，学生不仅学会了倾听，学会了赞美，学会了批评，而且还展现了自我、认识了自我，使个性得到了和谐健康地发展，同时也养成了他们的合作精神。本课在 Activate 的环节能够很快地让学生将注意力集中起来，借助学生的竞争意识，发挥学生的主动性，课堂一下子就活跃起来。通过对 Item 1 的学习，大部分学生能掌握文章中的重点词汇和句型，能够运用到自己的语言中去。在最后一个环节的 role-play 游戏中，每个小组的学生群策群力，闪现出学生创造性的思维成果。

Teaching Plan of First Letters

教师：许妍琼

Teaching Aim:

1. To get the students to know how to fill in the blanks with the help of first letters.
2. To get the students to practice first letters.

Teaching Objects:

The students in Class Five, Junior Three.

Language Points:

1. Ways to improve the skill of filling the blanks with first letters.
2. Practice with words, sentences and passages.

Teaching Aids:

Blackboard, chalk, and multi-media teaching aid.

Teaching Methods:

Task-based Approach.

Teaching Procedures

	Guessing Game Ask the students to guess the words with the help of first letters. The clues will be given if necessary. The students should spell the words correctly. e.g.: It begins with "l". It is a fruit. Answer: lemon

***A**ctivate* 在课堂教学开始前的较短时间内灵活安排新颖的导入活动，促使全班学生集中注意力，迅速进入学习状态。	The student who gets the most answers will win and get a prize. Ask the winner to guess what the prize is. It begins with “l”. (lollipop) lemon It begins with “l”. It is a fruit.
***B**uild* 运用综合教学方法指导教学设计，营造良好的学习氛围，使学生快乐、自然、轻松、有效地学习语言。	**Practice with sentences.** The sentences will be divided into 4 groups. The first group is about collocation. e.g.: There's no p<u>roblem</u> so hard that we can't solve it together. The second group is about general knowledge. e.g.: Christopher Columbus discovered A<u>merica</u> in 1492. The third group is about context. e.g.: I really p<u>ity</u> her. She has had such a hard life. The fourth group is about correct forms. e.g.: On her wedding day she s<u>miled</u> happily in all the photographs. Group 1 1. I'd love to show you round the city—can I be your tourist g<u>uide</u>? 2. You need a large a<u>mount</u> of money to buy a house in London. 3. There is no p<u>roblem</u> so hard that we can't solve it together. 4. They are very f<u>riendly</u> to people and also very beautiful. 5. On Monday morning he got up at six as u<u>sual</u>.

Cultivate 按照启发式教学原则，设计饶有趣味的训练来充分调动学生学习的主动性。	**Practice with passages.** The students are given two passages to practice. They are supposed to use the methods that they have learned to fill in the blanks. Passage 1 School education is very useful. Many people go to school for education. They l__1__ languages, history, geography, physics, chemistry and math. Others go to school to learn a s __2__ so that they can make money. But n__3__ can learn everything from school. A teacher, no matter how much he k__4__, cannot teach his students everything they want to know. His j__5__ is to help his students know how to learn. He teaches them how to read and how to think. So, much more is to be learnt by the s__6__ themselves. It's always more i__7__ to learn how to study by oneself than to memorize some facts or rules. Great scientists, like Newton, Galileo and Edison, didn't learn everything from school, but they were all s__8__. They invented many things. The r__9__ for their success is that they knew how to study. They read books that were not taught at school. They w__10__ hard all their lives, wasting not a single moment. Above all, they knew how to use their brains.
Develop 设计真实的语言环境来综合概括构建及养成部分所传达的语言信息，巩固课堂教学、衔接新旧知识、贯通前后内容，帮助学生学习训练，复习巩固。	**Group Work** Ask the students to talk about how to get high marks in this part.
Evaluate 评估教学活动的实际效果，分析学习成效，帮助学生排除学习障碍。	Then fill in the blanks with first letters. Check if the students know how to finish this part in a good way. 1. Have a large vocabulary. 2. Be knowledgeable. 3. Know more grammar rules. 4. Understand the context. 5. Pay attention to word forms. How to get high marks in this part? • 1. Have a large vocabulary. • 2. Be knowledgeable. • 3. Know more grammar rules. • 4. Understand the context. • 5. Be careful to word forms.

课程设计及反思

教师：许妍琼

我的这节课是针对中考题型首字母填空的专项复习课，是一节任务型教学法贯穿始终的复习课。

我这节课的教学目的是希望通过完成关于词—句—篇章的各项关于首字母的任务，让学生掌握做首字母填空题的技巧与方法。我主要使用了任务型教学法。

第一步，在 Activate 环节中，做猜词游戏。在首字母的提示下，给学生想象的空间，再给出一定的提示，让学生们有限制地去猜。学生表现极其踊跃，争先恐后讲出自己想到的词。起到了调动课堂气氛的作用。同时，学生的思维也被打开。可以训练学生对于词汇的联想能力。任务教学法要求我们注意可操作性原则。在任务的设置上，我比较注意所猜词语的难度。难度太低、太简单，没有挑战性。难度太高，没有学生能够猜得出，又失去了意义。

第二步，在 Build 环节中，做句子首字母填空练习。我精选了很多句子，并将其分为 4 类，分别是固定搭配、常识、上下文理解、正确形式。每组各有 10 个句子，都与其中心内容相关。在每组的句子被给出之后，让学生自己总结这一组的核心内容。还是要求学生去完成任务——句子的首字母填空任务。任务型教学要求，在下达任务时，要让学生明确学习目标，在操作过程中把握知识点，在完成任务中指导解决难点，完成任务后共同小结，通过小结把任务中涉及的知识、概念加以归纳、系统化，并做适当提高。这部分的效果还是很不错的。在这些句子的实际演练中，学生无疑印象深刻，会对这四类规律记忆犹新。对于他们掌握首字母填空的规律和掌握提高这方面能力的方法打好基础。

第三步，在 Cultivate 环节中，做篇章首字母填空练习。经过刚才集中的句子分类练习之后，进行篇章的练习。这部分还是采用了英语教学的任务型教学法。让学生在这一环节运用刚才教师讲的一些解题方法。在这一环节，精选两篇需要运用到这些方法的题目。让学生在实战中运用以上的规律和技巧。

第四步，在 Develop 环节中，提出问题 How to get high marks in this part? 让学生思考这个问题，用英语表述出来。

第五步，在 Evaluate 环节中，用填空的形式来完成总结。

☞ 教学反思：

任务教学法，也叫任务型教学法，是美国教育家杜威以实用主义作为教育理论基础而提出的“学生中心，从做中学”的教学模式，他主张教育的中心应从教师和教科书转到学生，教学应引导学生在各种活动中学习。在课堂教学中始终围绕既定的教学任务展开，使每节课目的明确、内容实在、效果最佳。这种课堂教学模式，被概括为任务教学模式。

整节课以首字母的练习贯穿始终，遵循了任务型教学法的连贯性原则。任务型教学并非指一堂课中穿插了一两个活动，也不是指一系列活动在课堂上毫无关联地堆积。任务型教学是指教学通过一组或一系列的任务履行来完成或达到教学目标。学生从 guessing game 到最后的总结，都是以首字母的形式去完成的。最后的总结以简练的形式呈现出来，相信学生能够印象深刻。

这次复习课的尝试，应该说是成功的。通过这样的方式，学生再也不惧怕这样棘手的中考题型。通过这次尝试，也让我意识到，如果我们教师肯多花点心思，巧妙地设置任务，复习课也不会那么沉重，不会变成一节中文陈述课。而是让学生完全进入一个英语的语言环境中，通过完成任务去体会做题方法。让学生既享受了英语课的乐趣，又学到了复习课应该掌握的内容。

Teaching Plan for in *Look Listen and Learn* Book Ⅲ Lesson 29

教师：向丹

Teaching Aims:

1. To raise the students' awareness of expressing their own feelings with the command of the complex sentence structures as *so…that*, *too…to*, *enough…to*.
2. To elicit the students' right attitudes towards life.

Teaching Objects:

The students from Junior Two.

Language Points:

Sentence structures *so…that*, *too…to*, *enough…to*.

Teaching Aids:

A tape-recorder, and multi-media teaching aid.

Teaching Methods:

1. Task-based Language Teaching Approach.
2. Situational Teaching Approach.

Teaching Procedures

Activate 在课堂教学开始前的较短时间内灵活安排新颖的导入活动，促使全班学生集中注意力，迅速进入学习状态。	1. Greetings and duty report. 2. Guessing game—brainstorming. A game is designed for the understanding of and the comparison among *a little*, *so/very* and *too*. The teacher offers four pictures and asks the students to reply and guess the prices of those items by the representative's answering "*That's too high*" or "*That's a little low*", etc. The group with the closest price wins. This guessing game is served to tune them in the language of English first and then pave for the main topic in this lesson. Pictures offered here are used to elicit the differences and degrees among the three words. After grasping the main knowledge, a guessing game of the proper price is served. The brainstorming method is applied here as the students are required to shout out the price in their mind without much thinking.

a little happy
so happy
too happy

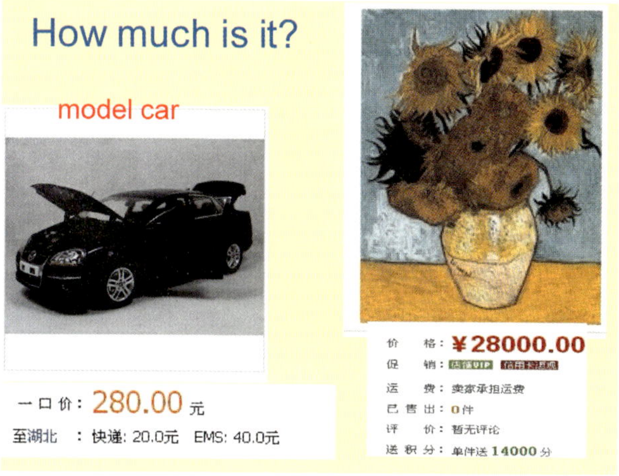
How much is it?
model car
一口价：280.00 元
至湖北　：快递: 20.0元　EMS: 40.0元
价　格：¥28000.00
促　销：
运　费：卖家承担运费
已售出：0件
评　价：暂无评论
送积分：单件送 14000 分

【晓岚阁】仿古房子模型
一口价：3800.00 元
运　费：平邮: 20.00元 快递: 50.00元 EM
30天售出：0件
付款方式：支付宝卡通　网银支
网点支付　支付宝
时尚创意 超可爱木质手绘荷兰风车鞋子摆设 家
淘宝网将保障您的购物资金及运费安全，查看保障须知。
一口价：12.00 元
促　销：
至湖北：快递: 10.0元
30天售出：0件 (已有-人评论)
付款方式：信用卡　支付宝卡通　网银支付　找人代付
消费卡　网点支付　支付宝余额

Build

运用综合教学方法指导教学设计，营造良好的学习氛围，使学生快乐、自然、轻松、有效地学习语言。

Get the students to know the sentence patterns *too…to*, *so…that…*, *enough…to*. The illustration of this phase is processed by separating and completing pictures that emphasize on individual sentences like *This is so* … and *They can't* … and eventually the whole sentences like *It is too…to…*, *It is so… that…* and *It is not… enough to…* The first two sets of pictures are elicited to be told with the help of the teacher and the left four sets are done individually by the students themselves.

The fish is too big.

big

eat

The cat can not eat it.

The fish is too big for the cat to eat.

The fish is so big that the cat can't eat it.

The mailbox is very tall.

The girl can not reach it.

short

reach

hard cut

- The steak was too hard for him to cut.
- It was so hard that he couldn't cut it.
- It was not soft enough for him to cut.

<table>
<tr>
<td></td>
<td>

hard
finish

- The homework was too hard for me to finish.
- The homework was so hard that I couldn't finish it.
- It was not easy enough to finish.

This part is based on the scaffolding teaching method. An old scaffold of the familiar sentence patterns are given and then the students are required to get the clues of the new scaffold and they will be able to make up sentences themselves.
</td>
</tr>
<tr>
<td>
Cultivate

按照启发式教学原则，设计饶有趣味的训练来充分调动学生学习的主动性。
</td>
<td>
Grasp the expressions, sentence patterns and main idea of the text.

- Listen to the tape with books closed for the first time. Answer the related questions in the text. This is for the overall understanding of the text.
- Listen to the tape again with pauses by sentence and the students are required to repeat with it. Emphasize on the pronunciation and intonation.
- Listen to the text for the third time. Choose some students to repeat it individually.
- Listen to it and fill in the blanks according to the text.
- Retell the story with the help of some hints like pictures or key words.

Questions

Where did the children go last week?
Who could lift a heavy weight? Why?
Could a clown lift a heavy weight?
What did he do later?
</td>
</tr>
</table>

Lesson 29 The Weight-lifter

Last week father took the children to a circus.
First they saw a weight-lifter. He was very strong.
He picked up a heavy weight.
He was strong enough to lift it above his head.
Then a clown appeared.
He tried to lift the weight, but he couldn't!
He was too weak to lift it!
Suddenly, the clown picked up another big weight.
He lifted it easily.
But the clown's weight was only a bar and two balloons!

Last week father took the children to a circus.
First they saw a . He was very strong.
He picked up a heavy weight.
He was strong enough to lift it above his head.
Then a  appeared.
He tried to lift the weight, but he couldn't!
He was too weak to lift it!
Suddenly, the clown picked up another big weight.
He lifted it easily.
But the clown's weight was only a bar and two balloons!

1. Create a certain situation and check if the students can use the sentence patterns freely.
   Given a familiar situation such as a guy complaining about his school life to his parents as a frame, together with some information as complementary material, groups of two or three students will response to it. The best groups which can use the sentences most fluently and most vividly win. Assessment is also needed.

Develop

设计真实的语言环境来综合概括构建及养成部分所传达的语言信息，巩固课堂教学、衔接新旧知识、贯通前后内容，帮助学生学习训练，复习巩固。

Act it out!

A boy named Picky is complaining about his school life to his mum Ms. Easy who is so easy-going. Make a dialogue with the sentences you just learnt.

(homework tests food noise light schoolbag...)

2. Moral education should also be given. *Is it necessary to make complaints all the time*? This is what the students should eventually learn from the text and the teacher. With reference to the clown who makes life funnier and easier, a part of a commercial ad. is served as a vital source. Watch the video for the first time and answer a simple question as what he lost in one day. The second task is for the students to make sentences connected to its context. Key words being shown already, the students are allowed to let the teacher pause from time to time so as to make sentences.

<table>
<tr>
<td></td>
<td>
Is it good to be picky?
A day too hard
What did the boy lose in a day?
1. boss rude bear
2. stationery heavy carry
3. car dear afford
4. gap(缝隙) wide lose

Sometimes life is too hard,
but we can make it easy enough.
</td>
</tr>
<tr>
<td>
Evaluate

评估教学活动的实际效果，分析学习成效，帮助学生排除学习障碍。
</td>
<td>
Assessment and Conclusion
Evaluate the students' performance and make a conclusion about life and our attitude.

Homework
An appropriate amount of homework is ought to be given as the conclusion from the students.

Homework
· Recite the text.
· Finish exercise about it in the workbook.
· Write out the rude sentences that you will last choose when quarreling with your mum or complaining about life.
</td>
</tr>
</table>

课程设计及反思

教师：向丹

本课选自课本《看听学》第 3 册第 29 课，该课文在英语学习中起到了非常重要的作用，教学目标是使学生由简单句开始过渡到对复合句的初识和掌握，到最终的熟练使用，并在日常场景中自如再现。本课程设计基于支架教学理论，其中运用了头脑风暴、情景教学法、角色扮演法等。

一、激活课堂氛围（Activate）

在教学开始前的较短时间内安排小游戏，促使全班学生集中注意力，迅速进入学习状态。

1. 图片比较

三张图片直观形象地说明 a little，too，so 的差异。学生由猜测到清楚意识到在不同的环境中应使用不同的形容词。

2. 价格猜测游戏

本环节使用了头脑风暴教学法。教师提供不同事物的照片，让学生分组猜测该物品的价格并不加思考地说出他们心中的估价，估价与真实价格差距最小的组获胜。每组派一位代表上台，组员提示。提示语必须包含 too，little，very 这些比较模糊的概念而非具体数字。汽车模型、房屋模型等的价格难以准确衡量，因此学生在此环节会加深对这些表程度的形容词/副词的了解，强化第一阶段的教学成果。

二、创建教学环境（Build）

此部分旨在运用综合教学方法指导教学设计，营造良好学习氛围，使学生快乐、自然、轻松、有效地学习语言，实现由旧支架向新支架的过渡（scaffolding）。

学生对反复出现的 a little，so，too 已熟练了解，在此环节中难度加强，包含这几个词的简单句通过图片形式出现，这是学生通过此前的课程已掌握的旧支架。教师在此加以引导，介绍新支架，即 too…to，so…that…，…enough…to 句型。展示第一幅和第二幅图时教师的主导作用明显，而其余的图片则由学生通过自己的努力和个别关键词的提示独立组句。新支架由此构建，学生也经历了由了解到描述图片的过程。

三、养成主动学习（Cultivate）

按照启发式教学原则，设计饶有趣味的训练来充分调动学生学习的主动性以促进课程主体的讲授（任务教学法）。

该环节是本课时的重点。任务教学法在这里得到了充分的运用。（1）初听：在初听课文前，教师要求学生合上书本，看清屏幕上的问题，带着任务听录音。（2）精听：初听后，回答问题，核对答案。然后进行一次跟读训练。再次关书听音，听音的同时，屏幕上显示填空任务。

四、发展综合技能（Develop）

设计真实语言环境来综合概括，巩固课堂教学、衔接新旧知识、贯通前后内容，帮助学生训练，复习巩固，拓展技能。

本环节运用角色扮演和情景教学法。制造生活情景，邀请学生扮演家庭角色并对校园生活进行评论，使用关键句型 too...to，so...that...，...enough...to。要求学生分组后自如运用所学的新支架完成任务。情感教育也穿插在本阶段的教学中。通过一段视频再次运用关键句型并调整学生在上一环节角色扮演后的负面情绪。视屏播放前提出与其相关的问题：这个孩子在这一天失去了什么？再次播放视频。要求学生依据所提供的关键词从视频中寻找相关句型。最后教师邀请学生进行引导性总结。

五、给予反馈评价（Evaluate）

评估教学活动的实际效果，分析学习成效，帮助学生排除学习障碍并巩固学习效果。此部分由教师对学生的评价、学生小组或个人间的对比组成。适量家庭作业的布置可以帮助学生及时巩固本课所学的知识点，提高综合能力。

Teaching Plan of *Look Ahead* Book 1 Unit 2

教师：张金霞

Teaching Aims:

1. Talk about personal information, jobs and places.
2. Advertisements for jobs.

Teaching Objects:

The students in Grade One.

Language Points:

1. The students are required to master the following words and useful expressions: address(es)(*n.*), boss(es)(*n.*), company(ies)(*n.*), country(ies)(*n.*), earn(*n.*), envelope(*n.*), everyone(*n.*), first name(*n.*), form(*n.*), job(*n.*), letter(*n.*), marital stature(*n.*), medicine(*n.*), patient(*n.*), person(*n.*), personal(*adj.*), picture(*n.*), postcode(*n.*), road(*n.*), salary(ies)(*n.*), street(*n.*), surname(*n.*), taxi driver(*n.*), town(*n.*)
2. Personal information: name, marital stature, telephone number, forms of address, postcode, places, title, nationality, jobs

Teaching Aids:

Tape-recorder, slide show, and picture show.

Teaching Methods:

Situational Teaching.

Teaching Procedures

Activate

在课堂教学开始前的较短时间内灵活安排新颖的导入活动，促使全班学生集中注意力，迅速进入学习状态。

1. Greeting and duty report.
2. Game: "Who has a good memory?"

   Ask the students to remember the jobs with the help of the pictures.
   a shop assistant, a builder, a cleaner, an electrician, a doctor, a driver, a mechanic, an actor, a secretary, a teacher, a nurse, a musician, a painter, a footballer, a singer, a politician, a cook, a baker, a butcher, a carpenter, a thatcher, an actress, a tennis player, a receptionist, a computer operator, an assistant manager, a sports teacher.

Build

运用综合教学方法指导教学设计，营造良好的学习氛围，使学生快乐、自然、轻松、有效地学习语言。

1. Presentation.

   Tell the students that we are going to learn a dialogue of starting a new job and another dialogue of talking about the names, nationalities, jobs, and so on.
2. Listening.

   (1) Now listen to the dialogue and find out this information.
   (Part 1 on Page 14)
   ① What's James' surname?
   ② Is James married or single?
   ③ Where is James from?
   ④ What's his telephone number?

   (2) Listen to the dialogue again, and complete the form.

Surname	
First Name(s)	
Marital Status	
Nationality	
Address	
Telephone Number	

3. Listening.

   Now listen to another dialogue and find out this information.
   (Part 7 on Page 15)
   (1) Rosie is from London. (T/F)
   (2) Rita is the managing director. (T/F)
   (3) James likes his new job. (T/F)
   (4) Tom Hall is James' boss. (T/F)

Cultivate 按照启发式教学原则，设计饶有趣味的训练来充分调动学生学习的主动性。	1. Personal information. (1) Name, marital stature, telephone number, forms of address, postcode, places, title, nationality, jobs (2) Forms of address Mr. , Miss, Mrs. , Ms. 2. Activities. (1) Match the words with the people in the picture. (Part 1 on Page 16) (2) Additional words and expressions about jobs. out of work, unemployed, jobless, housewife (3) Read and try to remember the details, and then fill in the blanks, according to your memory. My name is Mary Baker. I'm an English teacher in a middle school in Tianjin. My brother Paul is with me. We live in 18 Nankou Road, Tianjin. We come from London. My brother is single and he is applying the job as a computer operator. First Name ________ Surname ________ Marital Status________ Address ________ Nationality ________
Develop 设计真实的语言环境来综合概括构建及养成部分所传达的语言信息，巩固课堂教学、衔接新旧知识、贯通前后内容，帮助学生学习训练，复习巩固。	1. Listen to two people talking about jobs. Write down the jobs you hear. 2. Interview your partner. Ask questions and note the answers. (1) surname (2) first name (3) married or single (4) nationality (5) address (6) telephone number 3. Free dialogue making: Talk about yourself or someone in your family.

*E*valuate 评估教学活动的实际效果，分析学习成效，帮助学生排除学习障碍。	1. Look at the "Personal Information". Write down questions and answers to complete the conversation. Workbook Page 8, Ex. 9. 2. Look at an advertisement, and make up a dialogue of interview.

课程设计及反思

教师：张金霞

本课选取了《展望未来》第一册第二单元第一部分 Personal Information 和第二部分 Jobs，是一节以听说为主的课型。

这节课的教学目的：了解各种职业的名词，学会谈论个人信息。

在整个课堂教学中，我使用了游戏教学法、听说教学法、情景教学法和任务型教学法。

具体步骤如下：

第一步：Activate（激活）

首先是学生进行 Duty Report，这是每节课都要进行的常规活动，目的是锻炼学生的语言运用能力。教师适当的点评对于进行 Duty Show 的学生和其他听讲的学生都是一个很好的提高机会。

接下来是热身环节，我使用了学生喜欢的游戏教学法，促使全班学生集中注意力，迅速进入学习状态。先让学生争相说出自己知道的有关职业的名词，然后运用图片展示给学生更多的有关职业的名词，让学生以小组为单位进行"Who has a good memory?"游戏。学生们在轻松的气氛中快速记住了这些单词。为下一环节谈论个人信息埋下了伏笔。

第二步：Build（构建）

Build 环节主要运用听说教学法，分为两个部分进行教学。第一部分采用 Free Talk 的形式展开，鼓励学生们在教师的引导下尝试谈论个人信息：姓名、年龄、住址、电话号码、婚姻状况、职业、国籍等。这是一个以旧带新的教学环节，学生很自然地学习到本节课需要掌握的句型。

接下来教给学生更多关于个人信息的表达方法：姓氏、名字、邮政编码、头衔等。学生会更有兴趣，对于谈论个人信息更加跃跃欲试。

第三步：Cultivate（养成）

这一环节是上一部分教学内容的延伸，按照启发式教学的原则，通过一个个任务层层递进完成教学。听说教学法和任务型教学法交叉进行。首先学生会听到两段谈论个人信息的对话录音，完成回答问题、完成表格和判断正误等学习活动，这些活动锻炼了学生在真实的语境中获取信息的能力。因为在 Free Talk 环节已为学生扫除了生词障碍，所以大部分同学可以很轻松地完成此环节的学习任务。学生在听的过程中对“谈论个人信息”有了深刻印象，为下一步指导学生“说”打下基础。接下来，采用连图、记忆游戏等一系列活动巩固职业名词和谈论个人信息等本堂课学习的知识。

第四步：Develop(发展)

我采用了情景教学法为学生设计了两种真实语言环境，以巩固课堂教学，帮助学生训练，复习巩固。

第一个情景是让学生两人一组对话，谈论彼此家庭成员的个人信息。

第二个情景是现场采访身边的同学，从姓名、年龄、住址、电话号码、婚姻状况、职业、国籍等方面入手展开对话，并要求采访者记录采访的个人信息。

通过以上活动，层层引导，鼓励学生们充分理解本课知识并融会贯通加以运用。学生可以发挥自己的想象力，不同层次的学生都会有自己的施展空间，保护了学生们学习英语的积极性，促进了全体学生学习能力的扩展与提高。

第五步：Evaluate(评价)

这一环节我引出《展望未来》配套练习册中根据个人信息表格编写对话，以及根据一则招聘广告编写采访对话两个练习，检测和评估学生对本课所学知识的掌握情况。最后布置了课后作业。

通过以上两种评价方式，我了解到学生对于课堂上所学知识的掌握情况。

☞ 教学反思：

本课一开始从 Free Talk 入手直切本课的主题，让学生迅速进入了轻松愉快的学习环境，大容量的记忆力竞赛游戏激发了学生的求知欲，快速抓住了学生的注意力，效果比较好。在本课的教授过程中，听说教学法、任务型教学法和情景教学法交替进行，符合十几岁孩子的认知特点。在学习活动的设计过程中考虑到了不同层次的学生运用英语的能力，整个教学过程中学生参与面很广，课堂气氛活跃。不足之处：这节课的容量有些大，如果删去“第三步 Cultivate 中的 3. Activities”效果会更好；教学中出现了关键知识点多次重复，学习程度比较好的学生会感到有些乏味。

教学过程就是一个不断反思、不断积累、不断进步和不断成长的过程。

归纳交际型语法教学法

归纳交际型语法教学法

李 雯

传统的英语语法教学往往采取以教师为中心的课堂教学模式，使得英语教学很难实现交际的目的，这与新课标培养学生综合语言运用能力的目标相背离。而外校的语法教学是在“教师主导，学生主体”的理念指导之下积极鼓励学生学会自主归纳学习，并结合任务型交际活动法进行语法教学。

一、基本概念

归纳法即教师先向学生逐步渗透具体的语言现象，然后让学生观察、分析并找出规律，归纳和总结出语法规则，这样就能使语法知识更容易被学生接受、理解和掌握。

归纳型教学模式一方面使学生能够自觉地收集信息并进行细致的研究，再将信息组织成概念，并学会处理这些概念。另一方面也是指教师利用一系列的学习资源让学生从许多个别例子中归结出某种原理或定律。归纳型教学符合教学内容的需要，所设计的教学活动多是先让学生从观察、体验中认识到某种观念的实例及特质，学生有较多机会从实践中学习。在这种教学模式中，教师的角色是资源的提供者及活动的带领者，主要是提供学习支架，引导学生学习。学生是主动的学习者，积极参与课堂的活动。这样真正实现了“教师主导，学生主体”的课堂教学。

运用交际法进行语法教学，就是要先简单地讲授英语语法概念，然后设置情景，开展交际活动，做到在教学中知识传授和能力培养并重，确保学生在交际中准确、流畅地使用英语。

二、理论依据

1. 建构主义学习理论

构建主义理论的核心观点：学习者要想获得成功的话，必须自己去发现和转换复杂的信息。建构主义理论将学习者看做是在不断地用新信息去检验已有的旧经验，并且当旧经验不再适用时，修改旧经验。由于构建主义理论强调学生是主动的学习者，因此构建主义的教学策略也经常被称为学生中心教学。在学生中心的课堂中，教师是“辅佐者”而不是“主宰者”，教师帮助学生去发现意义，而不是控制所有的课堂活动。所以，学习不是由教师把知识简单地传递给学生，而是由学生自己构建知识的过程。学生不是简单被动地接收信息，而是主动地构建知识的意义，这种构建是无法由他人来代替的。教师的作用从传统的传递知识的权威转变为学生学习的辅导者，成为学生学习的高级伙伴或合作者。教师是意义构建的帮助者、促进者，而不是知识的提供者和灌输者。学生是学习信息加工的主体，是意义构建的主动者，而不是知识的被动接收者和被灌输的对象。简言之，教师是教学的引导者，并将监控学习和探索的责任也由教师为主转向学生为主，最终要使学生达到独立学习的程度。

2. 教育心理学理论

教育心理学一个最重要的原理：教师不能只是给学生以知识，而应引导学生用自己的头脑来构建知识。教师可以通过多种方式来促进学生的知识构建过程，比如通过教学使信息变得对学生有意义，通过给学生提供机会，使之自主发现或应用某些概念，或者通过教学使学生有意识地、主动地将策略应用于学习中。教师可以提供“梯子”使学生通向更高层次的理解。当然，学生必须自己爬“梯子”。

3. 以学生为主体的教学模式

著名的教育家苏霍姆林斯基说过：“教师如果不想方设法使学生产生情绪高昂和智力振奋的内心状态，而只是不动感情的脑力劳动，就会带来疲倦。”英语新课程标准强调：课程从学生的学习兴趣、生活经验和认知水平出发，倡导体验、实践、参与、合作与交流的学习方式和任务型的教学途径，发展学生的综合语言运用能力，使语言学习的过程成为学生形成积极的情感态度、主动思维和大胆实践、提高跨文化意识和形成自主学习能力的过程。因此，在英语教学中应充分调动学生的主动性和自主性，让全体学生最大限度地参与到教学过程中，构建以学生为主体的科学教学模式。

由于空间及文化的差异，英语课堂教学活动要想取得高效，必须通过利用和挖掘学生自身的知识和经验，使教学活动内容更切合实际，也更容易被学生深切感知，从而提高学习效率。这种教学活动应该以学生为主体，在教室里模拟一个近似真实的情景，让学生在课堂教学活动中进行语言的操练。由于英语是一门实践性很强的学科，只有通过在真实的情境中运用，才能更高效地习得语言。

三、教学设计和实践

中学英语语法教学应该根据不同的教学任务、不同的教学目标、不同的教学时段采用不同的教学模式。一般来讲，教师教授语法知识都是在单元内容之后进行的，而不可能首先就对语法项目深挖细啃，花费大量时间去讲解操练。教师需根据教材编写者的编排意图，运用归纳法对本单元的重点语法项目进行专项突破。

例如，《英语综合教程》第四册第五单元把间接引语作为该单元的重点语法项目，于是该单元的主要语言素材中都有意识地、反复地呈现间接引语，使学生能够接触很多实例。教师除了引导学生观察教材中出现这类语言形式外，还可补充一些含有这类语言形式的典型例句，进而让学生发现这种变化形式，然后进行归纳总结，最后运用这种语法规则来检验学生对此项目的掌握情况。

在激活(Activate)环节中，教师主要使用了任务型教学法。让学生听一些以往学过的课文中的人物录音，猜测分别是谁所说的。然后给学生听一段间谍(含有直接引语变间接引语)音频，简单比较了一下两者的区别，就让学生试着将激活(Activate)环节里出现的直接引语变成间接引语。学生在转换的过程中会犯各种各样的错误，因此接下来教师结合例句引导学生归纳出将直接引语变为间接引语时需要注意改变人称、时态和时间、地点短语。再给学生大量的直接引语，让学生口头练习将它们变成间接引语。在构建(Build)环节里学生逐渐由不太会到基本掌握直接引语到间接引语的转换。

中学阶段的语法教学建议更多地使用归纳法，归纳法能推动学生主动参与，有利于学生观察、思维、分析等综合能力的培养，有利于学生探究学习和自主学习能力的提高。不过根据新课标的要求，语法教学绝不能止于仅仅让学生能发现、归纳出语言形式和规则，教师还必须向前迈出一步，那就是认真设计实际运用环节的教学活动。任何语言形式只有通过实践才能加深理解，只有通过实际运用，特别是通过在实际交际活动中去运用才能内化其规则、才能真正掌握。

在养成(Cultivate)环节里教师给学生设置了两个任务：第一个是向朋友转述一段话，原话用直接引语给出，转述的话在关键地方设置填空，让学生注意改变人称、时态和时间、地点短语。第二个是让学生听一段自我介绍的独白，然后用间接引语回答教师关于人物的情况提问。学生在本环节将所学知识应用到了实际的任务中，不仅加深了他们对间接引语变化规则的印象，更使他们了解到间接引语应如何在实际生活中灵活运用。

在最后的发展(Develop)环节教师给学生设置了一个将间接引语变回直接引语的任务。给出了一段用间接引语写的三人之间的对话，要求学生三人一组将其转换成直接引语并表演出来。在完成前面直接引语变间接引语练习的基础上，学生格外注意人称、时态和时间、地点短语的变化。这种倒置的练习增强了学习的趣味性，也使学生对直接引语和间接引语这一知识点掌握得更牢固。

在上述语法的教学过程中，学生通过分析、比较和练习若干语句，既能很快理解间接引语的用法，又能掌握间接引语的变化规则。之后，教师再通过反复操练，培养学生对语法规则的复用和活用能力。这样的语法归纳教学能使学生充分理解和内化语法规则，并使他们逐步构建起清晰且完整的语法知识图式。

四、归纳交际型教学法的优点与不足

归纳教学法就是通过有意识的教学设计来安排语法内容，创设一定的语法情景来激发学生主动学习语法知识，使得语法项目生动起来。另外，归纳教学法中的列举、分类等也正凸显了语法的语用本质。总之在归纳教学法的语法课上学生有足够的活动空间，这有利于学生学习能力的提高和学习策略的培养。

归纳作为一种从感性认识到理性认识的学习方法要求教师先给学生一些含有语法教学内容的语言材料，让学生在学习语言材料的过程中接触这些语法现象，然后引导学生从这些语言材料中归纳总结出语法规则。它能够让学生先获得语言材料，从感性认识中获得理性认识，有利于学生理解和掌握语法规则，但需要一定的教学时间，需要教师做比较多的语言材料的教学整理，而且在语言材料教与学中需要从语境、语用的角度进行教学，而不是直接从语法概念和语法规则出发进行教学。

交际教学法的优点是注重培养学生的语言运用能力和学以致用的意识，有利于激发学生的学习兴趣、钻研精神和自学能力，强调学生的主动性和相互作用，教给学生的是实际生活中应用语言的技巧。

但是，交际法也存在弊端。首先，以功能为主编写教材，打乱了语法本身的系统，增加了学习语法的难度。其次，同一功能可用多种形式表达，如何选择和取舍，没有客观的标准。此外，交际法对教师提出了更高的要求，如在备课方面和纯专业技能方面，对如何把握时机和方法加以有效的干预，要求教师具备更强的应变能力；教师还必须在外语方面具有较强的综合运用能力；交际法无法给教师提供使用教材的安全感。因此，在使用交际法时教师有必要选择、改写和自编他们所用的教材。

不同的教学法在语法的传授方法和对其重要性的认识上存在着差异。应针对不同的学生、不同的教材、不同的培养目标，采用不同的教学方法，最大限度地发挥其长处，以达到最佳的教学效果。根据我国英语教学的实际情况和现状，英语教学应博采众长、建立一种归纳法与交际法相结合的教学模式，即采用“归纳交际法”进行英语语法教学。一方面发挥语法教学的优势，培养学生分析语言现象的能力，掌握语言体系，提高教学效果。另一方面，充分认识到英语是一种交际工具，英语教学的目的是培养学生具有使用这种交际工具的能力，从而使学生的语言能力和交际能力同时得到提高。

Teaching Plan of Indirect Speech

教师：李雯

Teaching Aims:

1. To get the students to practice how to change direct speech into indirect speech.
2. To get the students to know how to report someone's words.

Teaching Objects:

The students in Class One, Junior Three.

Language Points:

1. The changing of pronouns in indirect speech.
2. The changing of tense in indirect speech.
3. The changing of time and place expressions in indirect speech.

Teaching Aids:

Multi-media teaching aid.

Teaching Methods:

1. Audio-visual Method.
2. Communicative Approach.
3. Task-based Approach.

Teaching Procedures

	Step 1　Warming-up T: Good morning, everyone! Can you recite Hobbies and Pastimes together? You have good memory, don't you? Now use your memory and play the first game of today. Guess who it is and what he / she says!

<table>
<tr>
<td>

A ctivate

在课堂教学开始前的较短时间内灵活安排新颖的导入活动，促使全班学生集中注意力，迅速进入学习状态。

</td>
<td>

You'll hear some sentences spoken by the people in our textbook. Please tell me after each sentence who it is and what he or she says. If you know the answer, put up your hand, please.

Game 1　Guess who it is and what he / she says!

Play the mp3 one by one. After each sentence, ask a student to say who it is and what he / she says.

Keys: Billy: I've got number thirteen.
Mrs. Boffin: It is cement.
Mother: I am making some sandwiches for tea.
Professor Boffin: I am going to weigh myself on this weighing machine.
Father: Where are my glasses, Sue?
Tom: Silly Billy can't touch his toes.
Sue: Can I make a boat like that?
Mr. Green: Don't forget your change.
Miss Williams: Whose is this exercise-book?
Sandy: Hold this kite for me please, Sue.
Fran: Everyone is sure she will win.
S. T. Zhang: We'd like to be away for about three weeks.
Lingling: There's just so much to see and do here.

</td>
</tr>
<tr>
<td>

B uild

运用综合教学方法指导教学设计，营造良好的学习氛围，使学生快乐、自然、轻松、有效地学习语言。

</td>
<td>

Step 2　Practice

T: Now listen to this conversation among three people. They are two spies and they are talking to their boss about someone they met at a party. Listen and answer this question: Did both the spies get the same information or different information about Agent X?

Play the mp3.

Did both the spies get the same information or different information about Agent X?

SPY A	SPY B
■ She said: I'm from France.	■ She told me she was from Spain.
■ She said: I own a shoe shop.	■ She mentioned that she owned a café.
■ She said: I'm married.	■ She said that she was divorced.

</td>
</tr>
</table>

- Agent X: I'***m*** from Spain.
  She told me she ***was*** from Spain.
- Agent X: I ***own*** a café.
  She mentioned that she ***owned*** a café.
- Agent X: I'***m*** divorced.
  She said she ***was*** divorced.

T: When we want to talk about what someone said, we can use the exact words. For example, Agent X said: **I'm** from Spain. Or we can use reported speech: **She told me she was from Spain.**
When we report what someone said we usually put the verb back one tense. So, for example, if the direct speech words are in the present tense, in reported speech the verb is in the past tense. Here's the direct quote: Agent X: **I own a café**. But when it's reported, the verb is in the past simple. **She mentioned that she owned a café**. Agent X: **I'm divorced**. Reported as **She said she was divorced**.
Billy said: *I*'ve got number thirteen. If you want to report what Billy said to someone else, what will you say?

Ask the students to change the sentences in Step 1.
Keys: Billy: *I*'ve got number thirteen.
→ Billy said that *he* had got number thirteen.
Mother: *I* am making some sandwiches for tea.
→Mother said that *she* was making some sandwiches for tea.
S. T. Zhang: *We*'d like to be away for about three weeks.
→ S. T. Zhang said that *they* would like to be away for about three weeks.

Professor Boffin: *I* am going to weigh *myself* on this weighing machine.

→ Professor Boffin said that *he* was going to weigh *himself* on that weighing machine.

Mrs. Boffin: It *is* cement.

→ Mrs. Boffin said that it *was* cement.

Tom: Silly Billy *can*'t touch his toes.

→ Tom said that silly Billy *could*n't touch his toes.

Fran: Everyone *is* sure she *will* win.

→ Fran said that everyone *was* sure she *would* win.

Lingling: There's just so much to see and do *here*.

→ Lingling said there was just so much to see and do *there*.

Sue: Can I make a boat like that?

→ Sue asked *if / whether* she could make a boat like that.

Father: Where are my glasses, Sue?

→ Father asked Sue *where his glasses were*.

Miss Williams: Whose is this exercise-book?

→ Miss Williams asked *whose* that *exercise-book was*.

Sandy: Hold this kite for me please, Sue.

→ Sandy *asked* Sue *to* hold that kite for him.

Mr. Green: Don't forget your change.

→ Mr. Green *told* Sue *not to* forget her change.

Step 3 Conclusion on Grammar Rules & Practice

T: So, when transforming statements, you need to check whether you have to change the tense. Let's look at some more examples.

Direct Speech	Indirect Speech
"I am tired," she complained.	She complained that she was tired.
"The exhibition finished last week," explained Richard.	Richard explained that the exhibition finished the week before.
"I've won the match already," shouted our friend.	Our friend shouted that he had won the match already.
"We're watching a football match," they told me.	They told me that they were watching a football match.
"I'll play tennis with Jane," she said.	She said that she would play tennis with Jane.
He said, "I am going to school tomorrow."	He said that he was going to school next day.

Ask the students to changed the sentences in direct speech into indirect speech.

T: Can you report what he said?

He said, "I live in Paris."
→ He said that he lived in Paris.
He said, "I am cooking dinner."
→ He said that he was cooking dinner.
He said, "I have been to London twice."
→ He said that he had been to London twice.
He said, "I visited New York last week."
→ He said that he had visited New York the week before.
He said, "I am going to find a new job."
→ He said that he was going to find a new job.
He said, "I will give Jack a call."
→ He said that he would gave Jack a call.
He said, "I can come tonight."
→ He said that he could go that night.
He said, "I may buy a new car."
→ He said that he might buy a new car.
He said, "I have to give Ken a call."
→ He said that he had to give Ken a call.

T: When transforming statements, you also need to check whether you have to change pronouns.

Now look at some examples and pay attention to the pronouns in the following sentences.

Pronoun

"*You* are too noisy," Peter told them.
→Peter told them that *they* were too noisy.
He said, "*I* enjoyed *myself* at the party."
→He said that *he* enjoyed *himself* at the party.
"*I* like *your* tie," she told John.
→She told John that *she* liked *his* tie.
"*You* know *my* husband," she said to Tom.
→She said to Tom that *he* knew *her* husband.

T: We also need to change time and some other expressions in indirect speech. Check out the following examples.

Time Expressions

He said, "I'm very busy *today*."

→He said that he was very busy *that day*.

The teacher told the students, "You will learn two lessons *this week*."

→ The teacher told the students that they would learn two lessons *that week*.

Mother asked me, "What are you doing *now*?"

→ Mother asked me what I were doing *then*.

"I'll do it *tomorrow*," he promised.

→He promised that he would do it *the next day*.

"I'm starting *the day after tomorrow*, mother," he said.

→ He told his mother that he was starting *in two days' time*.

I asked my brother, "Shall we go to the Summer Palace *next Sunday*?"

→ I asked my brother if we should go to the Summer Palace *the next Sunday*.

"I saw her *yesterday*," he said.

→ He said that he'd seen her *the day before*.

She said, "My grandfather died *three years ago*."

→ She said that her grandfather had died *three years before*.

My father said, "I bought you a dictionary *last week*."

→ My father said that he had bought me a dictionary *the week before*.

Other Expressions

He asked me, "How can I *come here*?"

→ He asked me how he could *go there*.

The teacher asked me, "Why haven't you learned *these* new words?"

→ The teacher asked me why I hadn't learned *those* new words.

T: Do you often speak to your mother on the phone call?

I'm going to play a phone conversation William had with his mother last week about his evening plan. After this phone call you'll hear him talking about the phone call with Jackie. Listen carefully and then tell me when he speaks to Jackie, does he repeat his mother's words exactly or does he change his mother's words?

Play the mp3.

T: Here's William's mum's original question:

William's mum: **Are you and Jackie coming over for tea?**

And here's William's report to Jackie:

William: **She asked if we were going over for tea.**

William used "if" or "whether" for yes / no questions. But if there's a question word, such as "who", "what" or "how", use it! And use "asked" instead of "said".

William's mum: **How are you going to get here?**

William: **She also asked how we were going to get there.**

William changed the pronouns, from "you and Jackie" to "we". And you have to use statement word order. William's mum said "are you", but William said "we were".

Now let's practice how to report questions.

Read the original question. Then complete the reported questions.

1. "Is it your birthday this month?"
   She asked me if it was my birthday this month.
2. "Are you having a party?"
   She wanted to know if I was having a party.
3. "Who are you going to invite to the party?"
   She asked me who I was going to invite to the party.
4. "Have you chosen the music for the party?"
   She wanted to know whether I had chosen the music for the party.
5. "What do you want for a present?"
   She asked me what I wanted for a present.

T: We've practiced reported question. Now, can you answer the phone and speak to your friend's mother. Say that your friend is busy. If she has any questions, please tell your friend what the questions are, using "She asked ..."

e.g.: T: Hello!
S: Hello!
T: Is Martin there? It's his mother.
S: Sorry, he's busy now.
T: OK! Did he have breakfast this morning?
Some alternative questions:
Has she finished all her homework?
How is he?
Why hasn't he called me?
What is he busy doing?

Step 4 Activities

1. Tell me what Frank told you.

T: These are the exact words Frank said to you yesterday.

"I've just got engaged! We're getting married next year. We're going to Paris for our honeymoon. It's all going to be very expensive. Luckily, my friend is a photographer so he he'll take the photos for us. We'll have the reception in my parents' back garden. My mum is baking the cake for us and my sister's band is playing free for us. I hope you'll come to the wedding."

T: Now you're telling your friend what Frank told you.

He said he ________ just got engaged. He told me that he ________ getting married the next year. He told me ________ going to Paris for their honeymoon. He mentioned that it ________ be very expensive. He said that his friend ________ a photographer and he ________ the photos for them. He mentioned that they ________ the reception in his parents' garden. He said his sister's band ________ free for them. He said he ________ I'd come to the wedding.

Keys: had; was; they were; was going to; was; would; would have, was playing; hoped

2. I am a SPY

T: We'll have a role play. We heard some spies talking before, but I need to tell you that you are also a spy and I'm your boss. And you met Agent Z last night, and he told you some information. I am going to ask you some questions about Agent Z and you have to tell me what he have told you and use reported speech. Listen to Agent Z now. This is what he told you. This is what his actual words.

Play the mp3.

T: So tell me. Did he say anything about his family? Where does he live? Did he mention any pastimes?

Keys: Yes, he said that he was married and had a child. He said that he lived in West London. He said that he loved traveling.

Cultivate

按照启发式教学原则，设计饶有趣味的训练来充分调动学生学习的主动性。

*D*evelop 设计真实的语言环境来综合概括构建及养成部分所传达的语言信息，巩固课堂教学、衔接新旧知识、贯通前后内容，帮助学生学习训练，复习巩固。	**Step 5　Development** T：Put the following paragraph into direct speech. Then make a dialogue in group of three. Peter introduced me to Jack who said he was pleased to meet me. I replied that it was my pleasure, and that I hoped Jack was enjoying his stay in London. He said he thought London was a beautiful city, but that it rained too much. He said that he had been staying in London for three weeks, and that it hadn't stopped raining since he had arrived. Of course, he said, this wouldn't have surprised him if it hadn't been July! Peter replied that he should have brought warmer clothes. He then continued by saying that he was going to fly to Hawaii the following week, and he said that he couldn't wait to enjoy some sunny weather. Both Jack and I said that Peter was a lucky person. Ask a group or two to come to the front of the class and perform their dialogue. Then give comments.
*E*valuate 评估教学活动的实际效果，分析学习成效，帮助学生排除学习障碍。	**Homework** Ask your partner the following questions and take good notes. After you have finished the questions, write a report about your partner in indirect speech with "He / She said ..." Questions：What is your hobby? What do you usually do in your spare time? Have you ever been to London? When did you go there? What are your plans for your next vacation?

课程设计及反思

教师：李雯

我的这节课选取了《综合英语教程》第四册第五单元的 Getting Started 部分。这是一节语法课。

这节课的教学目的是让学生练习将直接引语变成间接引语，让学生学会如何报告别人所说的话。我使用了语法教学法和任务型教学法。

在激活(Activate)环节中，我主要使用了任务型教学法。让学生听一些课文中的人物录音，猜测分别是谁所说的。因为人物是选自学生熟悉的课文，因此学生的参与性很高。

然后我给学生听了一段有直接引语和间接引语的音频，简单比较了一下两者的区别，就让学生试着将激活(Activate)环节里出现的直接引语变成间接引语。学生在转换的过程中会犯各种各样的错误，因此接下来我结合例句指出将直接引语变为间接引语要注意改变人称、时态和时间、地点短语。给学生大量的直接引语，让学生口头练习将它们变成间接引语。学生在构建(Build)这一环节里接触到大量的例句并进行了充分的练习，逐渐由不太会过渡到基本掌握直接引语和间接引语的转换。

在养成(Cultivate)环节里我给学生设置了两个任务：第一个任务是向朋友转述一段话，我将原话用直接引语给出，转述的话在关键地方设置填空，让学生注意改变人称、时态和时间、地点短语。第二个任务是让学生听一段自我介绍的独白，然后用间接引语回答教师关于人物情况的提问。学生在本环节将所学知识应用到了实际的任务中，不仅加深了他们对间接引语变化规则的印象，更使他们了解到间接引语应如何在实际生活中灵活运用。

最后的发展(Develop)环节里我给学生设置了一个将间接引语变回直接引语的任务。我给出了一段用间接引语写的三人之间的对话，要求学生三人一组将其转换成直接引语并表演出来。在完成前面直接引语变间接引语练习的基础上，学生格外注意人称、时态和时间、地点短语的变化。这种倒置的练习增强了学习的趣味性，也使学生对直接引语和间接引语这一知识点掌握得更牢固。

图书在版编目(CIP)数据

ABCDE 五步课堂教学模式及多种教学法运用之探究/徐涛,蔡文静本册主编. —武汉:武汉大学出版社,2011.11

武汉实验外国语学校 ABCDE 五步课堂教学模式丛书　李　茵丛书主编　王永汉丛书副主编

ISBN 978-7-307-08884-9

Ⅰ.A…　Ⅱ.①徐…　②蔡…　Ⅲ.英语课—课堂教学—教学法—中学
Ⅳ.G633.412

中国版本图书馆 CIP 数据核字(2011)第 123201 号

责任编辑:叶玲利　　责任校对:刘　欣　　版式设计:马　佳

出版发行:**武汉大学出版社**　(430072　武昌　珞珈山)
(电子邮件:cbs22@ whu. edu. cn 网址:www. wdp. whu. edu. cn)
印刷:湖北恒泰印务有限公司
开本:787×1092　1/16　印张:17.75　字数:397 千字
版次:2011 年 11 月第 1 版　2011 年 11 月第 1 次印刷
ISBN 978-7-307-08884-9/G · 2047　定价:98.00 元